GHOST INVESTIGATOR

Volume 5:
From Beyond the Grave

Written by
Linda Zimmermann

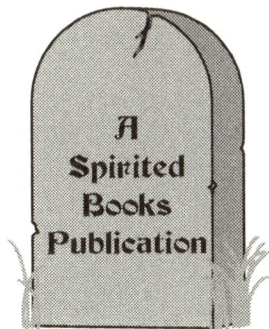

A
Spirited
Books
Publication

Also by Linda Zimmermann

Bad Astronomy
Forging A Nation
Civil War Memories
Ghosts of Rockland County
Haunted Hudson Valley
More Haunted Hudson Valley
Haunted Hudson Valley III
A Funny Thing Happened on the Way to Gettysburg
Rockland County: Century of History
Mind Over Matter
Home Run
Ghost Investigator, Volume 1: Hauntings of the Hudson Valley
Ghost Investigator, Volume 2: From Gettysburg, PA to Lizzie Borden, AX
Ghost Investigator, Volume 3
Dead Center
Rockland County Scrapbook
Ghost Investigator, Volume 4: Ghosts of New York and New Jersey

The author is always looking for new ghost stories. If you would like to share a haunting experience go to:

www.ghostinvestigator.com

Or write to:

Linda Zimmermann
P.O. Box 192
Blooming Grove, NY 10914

Or send email to:
lindazim@frontiernet.net

Ghost Investigator: Volume 5
Copyright © 2005 Linda Zimmermann

ISBN: 0-9712326-7-9

CONTENTS

Introduction

The popularity of all things paranormal, and ghosts in particular, appears to have greatly increased in the past few years. As evidence of this, I was recently in Gettysburg where you can't walk half a block without someone trying to sell you a ticket to a ghost tour. And where battlefields were once deserted after dark, you'll now find crowds of people hoping to catch a glimpse of a phantom soldier.

This is all well and good, but it does present some problems. For example, one group of people at the Triangular Field in Gettysburg was conducting an "investigation" in a rather unique manner. They were sitting in lawn chairs while music played on their boom box and every once in a while someone would lift a camera over his head and snap a picture of the field.

They seemed quite pleased with the results of their armchair investigation, too, as they kept announcing the number of paranormal "orbs" they were photographing. The fact that the air was filled with lightning bugs, countless other insects, dust, cigarette smoke, and that there were dozens of people and multiple flashes from other cameras didn't faze them. They were convinced they were capturing images of the spirits of Civil War soldiers, accompanied by appropriate patriotic background music, and nothing was going to convince them otherwise.

Therein lies the dilemma—while it's great that so many people have enthusiastically embraced the possibilities of a spirit world, a whole lot of nonsense is now flooding the field of paranormal research. It's so tempting to think that every fuzzy orb on your flash photo is a ghost, or that scratchy sound on your old cassette recorder is a voice from the grave, but resist temptation and examine the evidence critically and honestly!

For example, orbs have bothered me for years. If you have read any of the other books from my *Ghost Investigator* series, you know that I have included photos of those fuzzy, round spots, but that I have often questioned their validity as evidence of the paranormal. I didn't know what they were, and no one had been able to provide a rational explanation. Then a few months ago, I found an interesting article on the FujiFilm website. There was a picture of a teddy bear in a chair, with several classic fuzzy white "orbs" around it.

This was not a haunted teddy bear the Fuji experts had

photographed. This was an example of a common problem caused by, "Flash reflections from floating dust particles." The explanation went on to say:

"There is always a certain amount of dust floating around in the air. You may have noticed this at the movies when you look up at the light coming from the movie projector and notice the bright sparks floating around in the beam.

In the same way, there are always dust particles floating around nearby when you take pictures with your camera. When you use the flash, the light from the flash reflects off the dust particles and is sometimes captured in your shot.

Of course, dust particles very close to the camera are blurred since they are not in focus, but because they reflect the light more strongly than the more distant main subject of the shot, that reflected light can sometimes be captured by the camera and recorded on the resulting image as round white spots. So these dots are the blurred images of dust particles.

You can reproduce this problem relatively easily by taking a picture right after you put away goods that create a lot of dust, such as feather bedding. In actual photography, this problem frequently arises in shots taken at construction sites, etc. It may also occur when it is raining or snowing. Compact cameras in which the flash and the lens are close together are particularly susceptible to this problem."

(For more information, please go to their website at: http://home.fujifilm.com/products/digital/tips/reflect/index.html)

Do I now think that every suspicious spot on a photograph is dust? No, but this illustrates how important it is to exhaust all rational avenues before rushing headlong down the paranormal highway. All of the evidence at a scene needs to be considered, and things such as orbs and EVPs (electronic voice phenomena) can easily be deceiving.

All this being said, I am very excited about this past year's investigations. The cases have been extraordinary, and I have personally experienced some mind-blowing phenomena. I have also been fortunate to meet psychic Cyra Greene, who has been able to add a fascinating new dimension to some of these cases.

I hope you will enjoy reading these adventures *From Beyond the Grave…*

The Paranormal Passenger

As a rule, I only take the time to investigate a place if the owner agrees to allow me to write about it. Then again, even a ghost hunter's rules are made to be broken, and I will occasionally look into a case with no expectation of ever publishing the results.

In November of 2004, I went to check out a house where a woman had died under tragic circumstances. While several family members had since experienced unusual phenomena, they did not want any details of the case to be revealed. I respected their desire for privacy, and was fully resolved not to write a word about it. However, something so remarkable happened that the owner agreed to allow me to relate that part of the story, and that part alone. (So please, don't even try to ask me for any other details on this case!)

I had concluded my investigation, and the owner—let's call her Mary—and I walked to the driveway. My car was parked on the left side of the driveway, and Mary's SUV was parked on the right, with the front of both cars facing the house. As she went to the passenger side of her vehicle to get a piece of paper to write down her email address, I opened my passenger door. I put my large case of equipment on the seat and gave the door a shove to close it.

Suddenly, from *inside* my car, came a loud, but muffled sound of a woman crying out! My brain had a split second of disconnect, and I tried to grab the door, thinking that someone was yelling because I was about to close her arm or leg in the door. The door slammed shut, and reality slammed against my brain—there *wasn't anyone* in my car! Yet the voice was so loud, so insistent, so terribly close!

My head was reeling and I staggered backwards. It was like all my neurons were firing at once, trying to make some sense out of what had just happened. This was no computer-enhanced, faint, fuzzy whispering EVP on a scratchy cassette tape. This was a clear, loud voice within two or three feet of my face!

Could there be any logical explanation? My mind raced to find one.

The tape recorders! That must be it, one of the tape recorders had somehow turned itself on. I pulled open the car door, yanked the zipper on the case and tossed equipment aside searching for the tape recorder I had used on the investigation. It was not on. My heart and head were pounding. Wait, I thought, I had brought another tape recorder, and even though I hadn't used it, perhaps it held the answer. I pulled it out of a side compartment, but found that it, too, was not on.

Standing there with a silent tape recorder in each hand, staring at them in disbelief, I fought with the idea that I had only imagined the voice. But no, it was definitely not my imagination. With no more than thirty seconds passing from hearing the voice to standing there with the tape recorders, I thought to call out to Mary.

"Did you hear that?" I shouted.

"Yes, you mean the woman's voice? Where did it come from?" she replied from about twenty-five feet away, on the far side of the large SUV.

"*From inside my car,*" I stated, the stress in my voice clearly evident.

Mary hurried over with a stunned look, and explained that she also had heard the woman's voice call out, and at first thought it must be someone in the neighborhood, although it seemed too loud and too close. She saw the tape recorders in my hands, and asked if one of them could have been the source of the voice. I explained that when I opened the case, I found that both of them were off. We further realized that even if the recorder we had been using had somehow switched on, it would have to have been rewound first in order to play back any sound.

The idea was far fetched—my tape recorder managed to rewind itself, then play back a brief section of tape, then turn itself off, all in the span of a few seconds? But then again, a disembodied voice in my car was not any more likely a scenario. Yet, I had to explore every possibility, so I hit the play button to see if the tape had rewound. There was the silence of blank tape. I then rewound the tape for a few seconds, hit play again, and heard the exact end of the recording I had made during the investigation—proving that the tape had not rewound itself, thereby eliminating it as the source of the voice.

As further proof, I rewound the tape back to a section where my voice and Mary's were clear, put it back in the case the way it had been, turned the volume up to its highest level and closed the case. Although our voices were audible, they didn't even have half the volume of the loud woman's voice we heard, and Mary never would have been able to hear it from the distance she was standing behind her SUV.

That was it then, there was no concrete, physical explanation for the woman's voice in my car. As difficult as it was to come to grips with it, if the normal world could be eliminated as a source, then it had to have originated from the paranormal world. While my mind still found that hard to comprehend, in my heart I knew it to be true, because I did not only hear the voice, I *felt* it. It hit me like a bolt of lightning and left my head spinning and my hands shaking,

Occasionally, people will come up to me at lectures and book signings and say that they can't understand why I have these types of reactions to paranormal energy. Invariably, such people claim that they would *never* be affected by *anything*, and they would welcome such an encounter because *they* could handle whatever the other world could dish out.

Yeah, right.

It's like this—think of all of those armchair football players out there watching the game on Sunday afternoon. They yell that the quarterback should have thrown more accurately, or that he should have seen the open man downfield, or that he should have scrambled out of the pocket before he got sacked. And when the quarterback gets up a little dazed and has to sit out a few plays, the armchair heroes declare that *they* wouldn't have been affected like that. Of course, *they* have no idea what it's like to have a massive linebacker plant their heads in the turf.

Similarly, these often young and inexperienced "experts" haven't a clue what it's like to have a genuine and powerful jolt of paranormal energy crash into you. It's startling, unnerving, and can precipitate both strong emotional and physical reactions.

Such was the case with the voice in my car. It had been completely unexpected. The actual investigation had not produced anything dramatic, and by the time I was in the driveway my thoughts were already on the errands I needed to run on the way home. My "shields" were down and I was defenseless. It was truly a shock to my system, on many levels.

Naturally, there were questions about the encounter—was the woman's voice connected to the tragedy that had occurred there? What was the woman trying to convey? And last, but certainly not least, why

3

the heck did it have to happen in *my* car, and was I about to drive away with an unwanted passenger!?

As for the first question, both Mary and I agreed it was most likely the voice of the woman who had died at that house—and Mary spoke from experience. She admitted to me that several months earlier she had heard an identical woman's voice—loud and close, but muffled and unintelligible, like someone trying to yell through a pillow.

So, I thought, *I'm not completely crazy after all. Not completely…*

On the second point, we differed. Based upon Mary's knowledge of the practical and down-to-earth nature of the woman, she believed that this woman was basically trying to convey the idea, "Thanks for coming, but don't come back."

Not only did this not fit the impression I had received, but there was another more glaring problem. I had concluded my investigation, I was in the process of leaving, and I had no intention of having anything further to do with the case. If a spirit wants to be left alone, the last thing it should do is call out to a ghost investigator from inside her own car!!!

To me, the only part of this that did make any sense was that someone was desperately trying to *get* my attention. And let me assure you, she did!

Which left the last, and perhaps the most compelling question— was the woman's spirit still in my car? If so, would I transport it back to my house? These were not happy subjects for contemplation, and I was reluctant to put any of these theories to the test.

Mary and I discussed the remarkable situation for at least ten minutes, and during that time there were no more disembodied voices—in my car, or out—so I took that as a positive sign. Finally, I got into the driver's seat, took a deep breath, and pulled closed the door. Blessed silence! I admit I drove away with some trepidation, but about fifteen minutes later I felt confident that I was not ferrying a paranormal passenger.

The next day, Mary called to make sure I was all right. She saw how shaken I had been by the voice. On her way home she saw an accident, and while she was relieved to find that my car was not involved, she continued to be worried that the entity had traveled with me and had startled me into driving off the road.

A few days later, the voice was still very much on my mind. We were again back at Grandma's House in Port Jervis, this time with

4

psychic Cyra Greene (see page 6). Near the end of our investigation that evening, I simply said, "I was conducting an investigation the other day and as I was leaving I heard a woman's voice in my car. I couldn't make out any words, but it was loud and clear."

Cyra did not hesitate to reply, "This woman wants to leave this location, and she literally saw you as the 'vehicle' for her to get free."

"Couldn't it have been the case where she was thanking me for coming, but telling me never to return?" I asked, and saw that she was adamantly shaking her head "no" before I even finished the question.

"No! She needs you to help her leave that location. She was crying out for help."

The next day I emailed Mary, telling her about what Cyra had said, and how it agreed with my assessment of the desperate, muffled woman's voice in my car. I knew the clock was ticking on this house, as it had been sold and was scheduled to be demolished within a week. While I understood that the family did not want to return to the site, I felt it was my duty to at least make them aware of the possibility that their loved one needed help to break free of the place.

However, the family members apparently had made up their minds about the situation, and I never heard back from Mary. Hopefully, knocking down the structure and clearing the site will release whatever entity lingers there.

To be honest, though, I have been doing this too long to have much confidence in that outcome. There are far too many cases where new houses inherit old ghosts. I would like to think that in this unique case, as the woman appeared capable of summoning a considerable amount of energy to yell quite loudly from inside my car, she may now have the strength and understanding to move on. That is a comforting thought.

I would also like to think that this will never again happen to me. After all, I'm a ghost investigator, not a paranormal taxi driver...

More On Grandma's House

For those who have read *Ghost Investigator Volume 3* and *Volume 4*, you are familiar with the ongoing saga of Grandma's House in Port Jervis, New York, where fellow investigator, Mike Worden, lives. For those who have not yet read about this house, it has a long history of unusual activity—specifically the figure of a man (who has been identified as a former owner), a dark unidentified figure, footsteps, objects moving, and overwhelming feelings of sadness and loss, to name a few. One of the most dramatic episodes to which I was a witness—in fact, a participant—occurred in the summer of 2004, when something was knocking on a wall, and then responded directly to me when I knocked back. (Just thinking of that again gives me goose bumps!)

Many things have happened since *Volume 4*, most notably an encounter Mike had late one night, experiences by his young twins, and a visit from psychic Cyra Greene. The following accounts are in Mike's own words:

"I had awakened one night sometime around 3am to use the bathroom. When I was ready to go back to bed, I turned and saw the dark figure of a man standing in the second floor bay window. He was no more than twenty feet from me and was facing towards me. He was dark and there were no distinguishable features. As soon as I saw him, he turned around and 'walked' very quickly into my bedroom. It was as if he knew that he had been seen and was trying to get away from me. After standing there for a good minute or two I had to brave going into my room and sleeping there the rest of the night—with the lights on, of course!"

"One morning after working the overnight shift I came home and checked in on the twins. It was about 6:50am and they were due to be waking up shortly. When I peeked in, Ryan was awake so I picked him up, changed him, and decided to lay on the spare bed in their room with him to wait for his brother to awaken. After cuddling with him for a few minutes he looked across the room and pointed towards the mirror. He repeated this a few times. Then he pointed directly across the room towards the closet. I did not think much of this until he pointed towards his crib and I noticed that the mobile was spinning slowly. The mobile is tied to the ceiling, not the crib, and is up high enough that I could stand under it and not hit it with my head. The mobile over the other crib was totally motionless.

More recently I was preparing the boys' breakfast while one played in the living room and watched the 'Wiggles' on video, and the other was in the playroom off of the dining room. From the kitchen I can see through the house into the dining room and living room, so I was able to keep an eye on them. While I was scrambling their eggs, Ryan came running into the kitchen very upset, saying 'Man! Man!' and pointing to the living room. I picked him up and he immediately hugged me hard, saying very softly, 'Man.' I carried him into the living room and checked that the front door was locked and no one was there. I calmed him and went back to cooking.

A few minutes went by and I heard him calling for daddy in an urgent tone, and as I went to check on him he came running to me and jumped onto my legs to cling to me, telling me 'Man,' over and over. I brought him into the living room telling him that there was no man and then he pointed to the steps saying, 'Man,' and moving his finger along the steps as if following someone going up. About a half hour later, after breakfast, I was in the living room with both boys when they became concerned about a man, pointed to the back door, and said, 'There.'

About a month ago I went into their room to get them after a nap and both pointed to the mirror several times and said, 'Man there.'"

These encounters follow a pattern that is now at least four generations old. To summarize: Mike's grandmother and mother witnessed a man standing by the front door, and both watched as the man then proceeded up the stairs. A thorough search found that no one was upstairs and the front door was locked. Mike's niece was terrified by the figure of a man looking at her from the mirror in the bedroom where the twins now sleep. It will be interesting, once the two boys get older and their vocabulary grows, to see if their description of this man matches what other family members have described over the decades—an older man with a bushy mustache, often wearing a long coat and hat. (This particular apparition has recently been identified by witnesses from a photograph of the first owner of the house, Judge Obidiah Howell, who lost his son at an early age and never recovered from the loss.)

While this haunting activity remains consistent among an ever-increasing list of new witnesses (or should we say victims?), could any of this be corroborated on a different level? What would a psychic encounter here?

I met Cyra Greene in October of 2004 when she attended one of my lectures. We spoke for a while afterward, and I immediately felt comfortable that this was a psychic with whom I could work. We arranged to meet at Mike's house one rainy and foggy evening in November, and it would turn out to be a most memorable night.

We had some equipment set up in the house, but I wanted to keep it simple when Cyra was at work so I could devote my full attention to what she was saying. While my husband Bob Strong, and Mike's family members were in the living room watching a remote video feed from an infrared camera in an upstairs bedroom, Mike, Cyra and I went upstairs with just a tape recorder. From photos in *Volume 4*, she was able to recognize the stairs and the section of hallway where the knocking occurred.

However, she had not yet read the full account of the haunting contained in *Volume 3*, so she was totally unprepared for the crushing weight of feelings that can assault you in the front bedroom—the room where most of the activity is concentrated, and where the sad feelings of the loss of a child have overwhelmed us on more that one occasion. I had mixed feelings about not warning Cyra, but if I told her about that room then it would weaken or negate the evidential value of anything she sensed there. I thought it best that she enter with a clean slate, but I had no idea just how potent an emotional impact the energies in that room would have on her.

Cyra chose to enter that room first, immediately referring to it as "the children's room," although she did not know that this was where Mike's twin boys slept. At first she just admired the way the room had been decorated for the boys, but strong feelings quickly swept over her.

"A lot of emotions in this room. Crying, a lot of crying. This is really, really, *really* sad," Cyra said, as tears began to well up in her own eyes. "I very rarely break into a cry when I do this, but this is *really* sad."

I told her that we had also experienced this heartbreaking feeling many times, and had shed quite a few tears of our own. She then thanked me for *not* telling her about this before so that her reaction was pure and spontaneous, but nonetheless I felt bad, as though I had set her up for a paranormal ambush.

"This *really* hurts," Cyra continued, connecting with the spirit of a woman. "They took her child away, she was helpless, almost like a slave."

Mike and I were both startled by this statement, as the grief over the loss of a child had been the predominant feeling we had both experienced here for years. Although we had always connected those feelings with one or two male presences, we knew it was multi-layered and could certainly include at least one woman.

"I think she was imprisoned here, she lived in her own sweat, her own juices. Some terrible cruelty went on here. But it's almost like a saint, this person, this woman, she handled it like a saint, like a…like a Teresa of Avalon in her cell."

I explained how Mike and I had repeatedly felt this loss of a child, and this confirmation gave Cyra the chills.

"Then you aren't surprised that I felt this terrible loss?" she stated more than asked. Then the emotions welled up to a point where her voice became unsteady and she continued, "This woman endured the suffering like a saint."

We discussed her impressions for several minutes, and I asked if there was anything we could do for the woman, but no clear answers were forthcoming from this lost soul. As we spoke the air got colder and colder, until we were all shivering.

"I'm absolutely frozen," Cyra declared, as the icy chill and emotional pain escalated. "Let me get out of here, I'm just so cold. And the sorrow is just so unbearable, so heavy."

We had all experienced enough of that room for one night. While we were shaken by the encounter, my curiosity took center stage. Who was this tormented woman imprisoned here? Had this cruelty occurred in this house, or in some previous structure that had been on this land? Whoever this woman was who had endured her suffering like a saint, she had left an enduring imprint on Cyra's mind, and several days later she felt compelled to draw the image of the woman who had touched her heart so deeply.

The three of us then went into the middle bedroom. Cyra experienced many "layers" of trapped spiritual energy there that stretched back for centuries. It seemed as though the place was built on some kind of paranormal fault line.

"You actually sleep in this house?" she asked Mike in disbelief, and then said with a smile, "I congratulate you!"

The face of a spirit? This is the image of the suffering woman Cyra sensed so intensely in the front bedroom. The original drawing is in color, with the bright region around her head, face and chest being yellow, and her clothing blue.

We all laughed, which helped to break the tension, but the pain and unease quickly seeped back into all of us. Two of the primary entities Cyra sensed were someone bedridden and completely helpless—possibly due to a stroke—and a vengeful female spirit she could best describe as being a "hag." The "terrible, terrible heaviness" from this hag began taking a physical toll on Cyra, to the point where she was nauseous, her hands felt numb and "useless," and she rapidly developed a headache in her right temple. Mike also said that "this was the worst" he had ever felt in the house, and he, too, had a sharp pain in the right side of his head. It seemed that whatever we were each capable of sensing individually was being amplified by the three of us working together. A mixed blessing, to say the least, under the circumstances!

Cyra then began explaining more about some of the origins of these hauntings, picking up again on the theme that this house is something of a paranormal focal point, or "vessel" for spiritual energy. She felt that battles or fighting had taken place here long ago, which left just one of the many layers that weighed so heavily upon us now. Cyra's nausea was reaching an uncomfortable level at this point, so I suggested that we move on to the back bedroom—not that I expected it to be much better, based on past history!

Mike found that as soon as he crossed the threshold from that middle bedroom and into the hallway, the pain immediately stopped, and much of the heaviness was lifted. Cyra also felt some relief upon leaving, but with no recovery time went straight to the back bedroom.

At first I sat down with my back to the small storage room off this bedroom, but felt very uncomfortable. Without saying anything to prejudice Cyra, I simply stood up and moved to a different part of the room. However, I needn't have been so cautious, as she was already fully aware of the intense feelings of unease here. Unlike some hauntings where one or perhaps two predominant energies pervade an entire house, it seems that in these three bedrooms there are distinctly different personalities and issues. Unfortunately, all of them are unpleasant!

"I don't like it," Cyra plainly stated. "I don't like it and I'm freezing cold again."

Mike explained some of the strange phenomena in this room—the dark figure, the presence of a child, the many odd sounds and sensations. It was difficult to completely relax when you never knew what might happen as you tried to sleep.

"Mike, I can't believe you are living here!" Cyra said with concern. "It's not healthy to sleep with such vigilance, without being able to let go. It's not good for your blood pressure."

The pervasive feelings of unease and the penetrating chill were not good for our health, either, and we did not linger in that back bedroom. However, the most unsettling part of the evening was yet to come—the basement. First we took a short break to decompress. Often during investigations—especially in cases where the effects are physical—it is wise to step away for a little while to ground yourself and clear your mind. Once we felt more like ourselves, in more ways than one, we descended into the basement.

Although the air temperature was naturally cooler in the unheated basement, it did not account for the unnatural iciness that hit us all again. The numbness in her hands that Cyra experienced in the middle bedroom also returned. However, the most compelling sensation was one that suddenly engulfed Mike. His voice breaking from emotion, he briefly explained that there was an overpowering feeling that the spirit of his grandfather was right next to him. There was no fear, but the intensity of the emotion was almost too upsetting to bear.

We spoke about his grandfather's death, and without going into too many personal details, the circumstances of his passing correlated to the images and sensations Cyra had described. While there was a great sadness, there was, nonetheless, the comfort of the fact that loved ones are never far from us. This was not the trapped soul of someone who could not come to terms with his transition; this was a loving grandfather wishing to briefly communicate his presence.

Fortunately for Mike, the experience was brief, although the impact was stronger than anything else that had preceded it. However, our focus quickly shifted as another icy chill surrounded us, but the character of this presence was different, unfamiliar. This time we all felt as if a fourth person was physically in the darkness of the basement with us, directly behind Mike, and he joked that he was *not* going to turn around.

"This is a gathering," Cyra said, deep in thought. "This is a gathering of personalities. This one is a very shaky person."

She went on to describe again the concept that this house was something of a focal point, a vessel or gathering spot for many lost souls in the area. As she spoke, I noticed something solid behind her and Mike, but in the faint light filtering through a basement window, I couldn't make out any detail. It was large, but didn't move, so I assumed it was one of the upright supports. I shifted my attention elsewhere for a moment, and when I looked back, I didn't see it anymore. I asked Mike to turn on his flashlight, and point to the spot where I thought a basement support post stood, and there was nothing. Had the darkness played tricks on my eyes?

I looked at Cyra, and she also had a puzzled expression.

"I thought there was a post right here," she said, pointing to the same spot where I saw the black, still shape. "I thought this whole time that there was something solid standing there."

Perhaps there was.

As uncomfortable and unpleasant as the experiences of that night had been, it turned out to be an extremely important investigation. Cyra had proven herself to be a valuable asset—someone who not only possessed a special gift, but also the ability to handle difficult situations and clearly articulate what she was sensing. It was also good to get additional confirmation for many of the things we had been experiencing over the past few years.

What remains unresolved, however, is how to clear this "gathering" of spirits from this house. It is troubling to think that Mike's boys may be adversely affected by the negative energies there. It is also no less troubling to think that lost and tormented souls have yet to find release and move on.

Tragic Figures

During my hectic Halloween season lecture schedule in 2004, I gave a talk at the Monroe, New York library. People usually come up to me afterwards to ask questions and share some of their experiences, but this night there was something new.

A woman approached cautiously, as if trying to avoid being seen by someone. She slipped a piece of a paper napkin into my hand while saying, "I can't talk now with my daughter here. Call me." With that, she left, and I looked at the piece of napkin and saw that there was simply a first name and a phone number. The scene would have been perfect for the opening of a spy novel, but there would be no need for fiction—this would turn out to lead to a very remarkable true ghost story.

I called "Susan" the next day, and she told me about some of the apparitions her family had encountered since moving into their 100-year-old Monroe home in 1999. The accounts were astonishing enough, but when she went on to explain that they had discovered information about the deaths of previous owners that matched the unique circumstances of some of the haunted activity, I knew it was just my kind of place.

We arranged for me to come by to investigate one early November evening. Unfortunately, there were factors beyond our control other than the paranormal—Mother Nature. While the prediction had been for rain, the reality was snow and icy roads. I deemed it prudent to postpone the visit, and arranged to go to the house one morning a few days later.

It turned out to be a place I had been driving by for over twenty years, as I have friends who live a short distance from there. The house had never called any attention to itself—I never thought, "Ooh, that place gives me the creeps"—which just further emphasizes the fact that you never know where ghosts will be found.

Susan and her two affectionate cats greeted me, and I began to record her story. When the family moved in, it consisted of Susan, her husband, a baby boy and a four-year-old girl. Almost immediately, they began experiencing one of the bedroom doors slamming shut on its own. No one would be upstairs when it happened and all the windows were closed, so that there weren't any drafts. The slamming was so forceful it would literally shake the house. They never discovered any explanation, and the phenomenon eventually ceased.

Then Susan began experiencing the sensation of a child standing "at her elbow." Assuming it was her daughter, she would ask, "What do you want?" When there was no response, she would turn and find no one there. This happened repeatedly.

There was also the sound of a child crying on the stairs—not genuine sobbing, however, these were very much "crocodile tears," as if the child was merely trying to draw Susan's attention. It worked, and although she would always go to see what was wrong, she would always find that her children were nowhere near the stairs.

On one occasion, Susan clearly heard a little girl's voice call "Mommy." She thought that her daughter had gotten up and was about to walk into her bedroom and ask for a glass of water or something. Her daughter did not appear, and the child again said "Mommy," this time with more insistence. Reluctantly getting out of bed, she went to her daughter's room and found that she was sound asleep—so soundly, in fact, that she was snoring. Clearly, the voice had not been that of her daughter.

While most of these early attempts to get her attention no longer occur, there was one incident more recently that was unlike any other. It was also more powerful and disturbing than all of the other incidents combined.

Between the living room and the dining room, there is a door with a textured glass window. They always keep that door closed when they are not using the dining room. One day during the summer of 2004, Susan was home alone, sitting in the living room on the couch, which faced the dining room door. Suddenly, a face was "peering" at her from the other side of the glass! It was definitely a child, as only its head and hands came up over the level of the window.

As disturbing as this was, the most unnerving aspect was that the child didn't appear to have any eyes, only large, dark "vacancies" as Susan described it. Unlike most of the other phenomena in the house that is generally benign, Susan "hated" the sight of the terrifying apparition and ran upstairs to get away from the awful feeling, and the horrible, hollow-eyed child peering at her.

Unfortunately, the haunted activity involving children is only part of the story in this innocuous-looking old house in Monroe. Shortly after moving in, Susan's daughter was looking out of the kitchen

The door where the apparition of the child with the hollow eye sockets appeared.

window and announced that there was a woman in their backyard. Susan rushed over to look, but the woman was nowhere to be seen. She asked the little girl what the woman looked like, and without hesitation she replied, "She was tall and straight and gray, but now she's gone."

Normally, a mother might scoff at such an account by a four-year-old, but paranormal rules seem to apply here. On many occasions while Susan was washing the dishes, she would see the top of someone's head as he or she walked along the back of the house toward the door. The window over the kitchen sink looked out to the yard, and she could see brown hair, but nothing else. The first few times she expected a visitor was about to knock on her back door. However, after checking and finding no one there the first ten or twelve times, she realized that this was no earthly visitor.

On another occasion while she stood by the sink, she sensed a presence. Glancing to her left, she saw a reflection in the glass doors of a cabinet. There was a woman standing behind her, perhaps 40-ish, wearing a floral print blouse. Spinning around to confront the intruder, she saw nothing but an empty kitchen.

Then there are the cats—not her two cats, but two others that suddenly appear and just as suddenly disappear back into thin air. There's a gray tabby and a white cat with black patches. They have been seen throughout the house and, less frequently, in the yard (near where they believe they found pet grave markers). Susan's husband has even felt a cat jump on the bed at night and curl up on his leg—even though they sleep with their bedroom door closed, without their cats. The most remarkable sighting was actually only a partial one—a partial cat, that is!

Susan's bedroom has a small alcove where she and her husband have a desk. One night when she was alone, her two cats started hissing and growling, and their hair puffed up as if they felt threatened. Their gaze was fixed on the alcove, specifically under the desk. Susan looked, and was stunned to see the back half of the gray tabby. The tail moved back and forth, she could see its hind legs and part of the torso, but the front half of the cat was missing!

She watched in amazement as the back half of the cat walked out from under the desk and across the bedroom floor. As it moved, it slowly faded from her sight. However, her cats could apparently still see the phantom feline, as their eyes followed something out the door. Then they chased after the invisible animal, still hissing and growling, clearly wanting to drive the unwanted animal out of their domain.

The cats—of the living variety—have also had other encounters. They have witnessed and reacted to events that might otherwise have caused Susan and her husband to doubt their own senses. One day there was a thumping sound on the staircase, which leads from the living room to the second floor. Susan's husband was sitting in the living room and clearly heard it; the cats were staring intently at the staircase, so they obviously heard it, and Susan heard it from the kitchen and went to investigate.

As she often places things on the steps so she'll remember to carry them upstairs, she thought something had fallen and was tumbling down. However, that was not the case. To her astonishment, she saw a round, white, fuzzy object bouncing in a controlled manner from step to step downward. The object appeared solid, and the surface seemed to have the texture of fabric. As it looked completely real—bizarre to be sure, but real—Susan struggled to figure out what on earth it could be. After it hit the bottom step with a solid thud, it bounced down to the floor, and vanished!

Susan just stood there staring at the bare floor. Her husband—whose view of the object was blocked—quickly asked what had made that sound. Regaining her senses, Susan explained that it was a bright white ball, but it had disappeared. This was not the answer her husband wanted. He couldn't believe—he wouldn't believe—that something that sounded so loud, so clear, so solid, could vanish.

Jumping up, he started searching the entire living room, moving furniture, examining every square inch. There was nothing to be found. To this day, even though he, Susan and the cats all shared the experience, he refuses to believe that there isn't some rational explanation.

If he found the solid fuzzy object on the stairs hard to swallow, he wouldn't have any easier time with the transparent fuzzy objects seen in the attic. On several occasions, both he and Susan saw whitish or brownish fuzzy balls of lights darting through the air in the attic and the attic stairwell. They were definitely different from the solid white object that traveled down the main stairs. Susan described them as looking something like transparent "tribbles" (the furry round creatures from *Star Trek*), and they reacted as though they did not like being seen and sped away and out of sight. They sound remarkably like the fuzzy patches of light often photographed at haunted locations, although it is quite rare to personally witness one. As for the solid ball that appeared to be covered in fabric—that remains a phenomenon in a category all its own!

Even though they did not initially share the knowledge of these paranormal occurrences with family and friends, it quickly became evident that the ghosts did not limit their activity to the fulltime occupants. Family members simply refuse to spend the night there any more. They will come to visit, but at night they'll go to a motel to sleep, and be back early for breakfast the next morning!

A friend of Susan's had an experience during her first stay there that might help explain the situation. In the middle of the night she heard someone sighing in bed next to her. It was a long, plaintive sigh.

"Then I felt a finger running down my left arm, a combination of a long fingernail-type of feeling along with the pad of the finger, going from my elbow to my wrist," she explained. "I felt that something was in the room with me, but I couldn't see what it was."

A similar experience later happened to Susan—the sigh, the touching, and the feeling that a man was sitting on the bed. As remarkable as all of these experiences were, however, the most incredible were yet to come.

One day Susan heard a rhythmic pounding sound. It was as if someone was hammering on the roof. Of course, it was a ridiculous idea, as there obviously wasn't anyone on the roof. When her husband came home that evening, she asked if the heating system could possibly be making a sound like someone was hammering. He didn't think so, and he was unable to find any explanation. Until the next day.

They attended the annual Cheese Festival in Monroe, and struck up a conversation with some residents familiar with their house. Without mentioning the pounding incident (or any other of the bizarre phenomena), Susan asked about the history of any previous residents. Much to their dismay, Susan and her husband were told that a man who used to live there died at the house—or more accurately, *on* the house. He was working on the roof when he had a fatal heart attack!

It is doubtful that it is merely a coincidence that within twenty-four hours of hearing the pounding sound, they met someone who knew that the previous owner had expired on the roof. Yet, there were to be more surprises to come.

One summer evening in 2003, Susan's husband was in the yard using his telescope. As anyone who frequently uses a telescope knows, there's less strain if you keep both eyes open while observing. He was doing this, when out of the corner of his eye he saw someone approaching him. The figure walked straight toward him, and in the darkness it looked solid. Assuming it was Susan, he kept looking through the telescope until the figure was within arm's reach.

Straightening up, he turned to speak to his wife, and came face to face with a terrifying apparition.

The figure was completely black, and appeared to have some kind of robe and hood that he only half-jokingly described as looking like it belonged to the Grim Reaper. He stood staring for several long moments into the dark, featureless face of this deathly spirit, and then it simply disappeared.

When Susan heard her husband coming in the house, she thought that it was rather early for him to be finished with his astronomical observing session. Then she saw his face and knew that something was terrible wrong.

"I just saw a ghost," he announced, looking so pale and shocked that she didn't doubt his words. After describing what he had seen, he added with considerable alarm, "What was it going to do? What would it have done to me if I hadn't looked up?"

Taking some time to calm down, he asked Susan to go back out into the yard with him to retrieve his telescope. It was certainly a reasonable request under the circumstances, and it is likely many people having just had such a fright would have left the telescope out there until daylight.

While there were no more dark, hooded figures to be seen in the yard, both Susan and her husband saw something else. As they stood in the yard, they saw blue flashes of light coming from inside the house, on the second floor. They were like flashes of lightning. By the time they came back in, the blue flashes had stopped, but they both had clearly seen them.

As most apparitions go, this one has to rank right up there with the most terrifying in appearance. Also making this case more unusual is the fact that the manifestations take place outside in the yard. While it is not that uncommon, most ghosts do seem to inhabit structures. Is there any evidence to support the idea of a property-wandering ghost at this location? More than one could have ever imagined...

While attending a party, a neighbor told Susan and her husband that a woman died in their yard! In fact, it was the daughter of the man who later died on the roof. They believed she was outside tending to her roses when she collapsed from a brain aneurysm. That could certainly account for some of the sightings outside, but was there any truth to the neighbor's report?

On the afternoon that I had interviewed Susan, I called my friend Jim, who has lived in the area with his wife, Pauline, for many years. I wanted to know if he had any old maps of the area that might show what was at this location a hundred years ago, or even earlier. As I always try to maintain a homeowner's privacy, I at first just told him the street, and general location. His next question floored me.

"Do you mean the house where the lady died in the driveway?"

I was speechless for a moment, and tried to recall whether or not I had mentioned that a woman had allegedly died in the yard. I realized I had not.

"How did you know that!?" I asked, dumbfounded.

"Because I saw her," Jim replied.

At first I was thinking that he had seen the ghost of the woman, but when he explained, I was even more amazed to find that Jim actually *witnessed* the woman dying! It was in the early 1980s, and he and his wife were driving down the road during the day. They saw a police car parked in front of the house, and two police officers standing in the driveway. A woman was on the ground between them.

As Jim was a member of a first aid squad, he stopped to see if he could be of any assistance. One of the cops said that an ambulance would be there at any moment, and the situation was under control. Jim stood within just a few feet of the woman, and while he could see that she was unconscious, he couldn't tell if she was still breathing. A few days later, the woman's obituary was in the newspaper.

Even after listening to his entire story, I still couldn't believe my ears. What were the chances that he would happen to drive by at the exact time that this dying woman was on the ground, and decades later I would be investigating the case of her ghost! I've known Jim and Pauline for over twenty-five years, and neither of them ever mentioned this story. Then I just happen to call about a map, and he gives me an eyewitness account of her death! Every time I think nothing more can surprise me, something like this happens.

I returned to the house one evening in December to conduct a more extensive investigation. Unfortunately, it started raining so I was unable set up the equipment outside, but I did get to check out the house more thoroughly this time.

I set up the infrared camcorder in the basement, and there were a few small bright spots moving around, which could have been some airborne particles and dust stirred up by the furnace. However, there was one that moved unlike anything I had seen before. Roughly about the size of a pea or a dime, it moved slowly through mid-air from right to left about five feet above the floor, and about ten feet in front of the camcorder. Typically, airborne particles move fairly quickly, but this odd one lingered, hung almost motionless for a moment, and slowly dropped toward the floor and out of sight. Curious, but certainly not conclusive evidence of the paranormal.

Other than that, nothing appeared on the remainder of the video footage taken throughout the house, or any of the photos. The meters were also quiet. It was kind of creepy when I was checking out the door where Susan saw the hollow-eyed child, but that was the fault of my imagination trying to picture such a horrible sight.

It appeared as if the spirits were not interested in making themselves known that night. In the months that have passed since my last investigation, things have remained quiet. There was some concern that everything would get stirred up when the old kitchen was being gutted for a full renovation, but even this did not prompt any activity.

For now we will just watch and wait.

Is this another case where attention focused on the plight of restless spirits has helped them to find some peace? Let us hope so, for the sake of both the living and the dead.

***

Just before going to press, Susan told me that they were going to be selling their house. Nothing at all unusual had happened for months, and she speculated that, "Maybe they just wanted someone to believe in them," and that now that their story is being told they have found peace.

With any luck Susan's next home will also be peaceful, but I have some reservations about that. The house they will be moving into is over 200 years old and had been used as a doctor's office.

Let's hope the doctor didn't make any mistakes that will come back to haunt Susan's family…

Upstairs, Downstairs

Life was normal for Gina growing up in Nanuet, New York. The house was a mother/daughter high ranch, which is a local term for a two-family house. In this case, Gina and her family lived upstairs, while her grandparents lived on the ground floor.

Life became paranormal in this house after the death of her grandparents.

Her grandfather died in 1986 after a long illness. He was 86 years old, and died in the house in his own bed. Four years later, her grandmother died, also at the age of 86. She died in that same bed, and obviously knew she was about to die as her body was discovered with her arms folded across her chest, and the sheets had been folded and smoothed out as if she wanted to present a good appearance in her passing. It was no doubt a disturbingly memorable sight, but nothing to compare with the other things that were about to occur as reminders that the grandparents were dead, but not gone.

The first incident occurred about six months after her grandmother's death. Gina was not living in the house at the time, and had just stopped by for a visit. No one was home, but when she opened the door to the ground floor she was hit with the powerful aroma of her grandmother's cooking. Her grandmother was Italian, and an excellent cook, and the smell of her food was distinctive and unmistakable.

"I wasn't even thinking about my grandparents when I entered the house," Gina explains. "And then that wonderful smell of her cooking hit me. But it was only there for a second. I took another deep breath and it was gone."

Obviously, this wasn't the case of cooking odors clinging to the furniture or carpets, as the smell would have been present consistently, not just one intense instant. Of course, one whiff of lasagna does not a ghost make—but there were many other unusual events to come.

Soon after, Gina's brother moved into the ground floor of the house and claimed that nothing happened during the next few years. However, he is a self-proclaimed skeptic, and there was at least one encounter that casts doubt on his claims of "no unusual activity."

One day Gina stopped by to pick up some mail. The only other living creature in the house at the time was a cat. She sat down on the stairs, looking at her mail and patting the cat, who was calm and relaxed, when suddenly she heard a door slam downstairs. It was the metal door to the workroom, which always made a characteristic sweeping sound as the bottom scraped across the floor as it swung shut. She definitely did not imagine the sound, as the cat's hair puffed out in fear and he bolted off to find a place to hide.

Certain that someone had broken into the house, Gina ran outside and checked the doors and windows. All of them were closed and locked. She then hurried back to her house and called her mother to report the mysterious intruder.

"Oh, we hear that door closing all the time," her mother said, much to Gina's astonishment. "In fact, it happens so often that I finally went downstairs and said, 'It's okay, you don't have to shut the door anymore.'"

This unusual pronouncement was directed toward Gina's deceased grandmother, who had quite a pet peeve about that door. She was always telling people to close it, and often left notes taped to the door to remind people to always keep that door shut. Apparently, even death did not end her obsession with closing that workroom door.

As the door was on the same level of the house that her skeptical brother occupied, Gina asked if he had ever heard it close. Surprisingly, he admitted that he had heard the door swing shut by itself.

However, he was very quick to add, "But it's easily explained...I just don't have the explanation for it."

Now there's a statement worthy of a politician! Skepticism is perfectly natural, but in this case, I think the line has been crossed into denial...

Despite Gina's mother asking that the grandmother's spirit leave the door alone, she was apparently still adamant about keeping it closed. Finally, as a last resort they took the door off the hinges and removed it from the house. However, grandmother's stubborn spirit wouldn't let that stop her, as the sound of the slamming door remarkably continued, even though there was no longer any door to slam!

You have to at least give this ghost credit for persistence!

The empty doorway where there was a metal door that Gina's grandmother insisted be kept closed—even after she had passed away!

Meanwhile in 1993, Gina's two-year-old son (who had an excellent vocabulary and language skills for his age) was having conversations with an imaginary friend. Then one day in the car he suddenly asked, "Where's that lady?"

"What lady?" Gina asked.

"*You know*," the boy insisted, as if the "lady" was someone his mother should have seen and known. "Where's that lady? Where's Leda?"

Gina was stunned—her grandmother's name had been Leda! Gina was certain no one had ever mentioned the name to her son, and there was no way he could have known that name. Unless, of course, Leda had told her great-grandson.

"I didn't know what to say!" Gina recalls. "I just told him I didn't know where she was, and left it at that."

In the summer of 1997, Gina's brother moved out, and she and her husband and son moved in. The boy immediately began complaining that someone was in his room and he couldn't sleep, but they thought it was just his imagination.

That December, Gina gave birth to a daughter and brought her home on January 7—the anniversary date of her grandmother's death. In fact, the baby's crib stood where the grandparents' bed had been, which was the spot where they both died.

Gina tried not to think about it, but just a few days later, something woke her up in the middle of the night and she found that the room was lit up. The light was coming from a doll that glowed when you pressed it, but it was standing in the corner of the crib and the baby couldn't reach it.

"I slapped the thing to turn it off and went back to bed," Gina said. "But a few minutes later I watched as the doll turned itself on again. I made my husband throw it into the living room because I couldn't deal with it!"

In the months that followed, her daughter would often become very animated, cooing and waving her arms and legs, as if she was happy to see someone, even though no one was there. As a toddler, she would often stand in front of an old sewing table, look up at something over the table and point and laugh and babble as if trying to talk to someone. The table happened to be the one piece of her grandmother's furniture that had meant the most to Gina, so it was the one piece she had kept.

Although the majority of the activity seems to come from Gina's grandmother, her grandfather might also be leaving little reminders of his presence. One night when Gina's husband was working the midnight shift, she was up late watching television. While the house can make noises when it's windy, this was a calm night.

"There was a sharp popping sound in the ceiling," Gina said, trying to find the words to describe the unique sound. "It's hard to explain, but it was loud and persistent, and it really started getting to me. Then behind me I heard the sound of someone flipping through magazines, thumbing through the pages really fast. I immediately turned around but the stack of magazines was undisturbed. It all really freaked me out."

Only after the sounds had stopped did Gina realize that it was the anniversary day of her grandfather's death.

The next morning, the family was eating breakfast in the kitchen. The sunlight was streaming in, and always caused bright reflections on the varnished wood trim in the hallway. Gina's husband—another confirmed skeptic—was facing the hallway and suddenly went white as a sheet.

"What's the matter?" Gina asked.

He replied that someone had just walked down the hall and into their son's room—someone dark and solid enough to block the bright reflected light. They checked all of the rooms and found no one, but even the skeptic was sticking to his story this time.

"I don't know what I saw," he declared, "But I know I saw it!"

Another skeptic in the family, Gina's father, also has had several encounters he can't explain, although unlike all of the other activity, this takes place on the upper level of the house. When he is snoring very loudly at night, he often goes into the spare bedroom to let his wife get a good night's sleep. Many times he has awoken to the feeling of a presence, and a very strong smell of perfume. This "old lady perfume" as he describes it, always smells the same, and only he has smelled it in just that room.

Gina's family bought the house back in 1967, and there had only been one previous owner—an elderly grandmother who just happened to have died in that upstairs bedroom! Skeptical or not, this seems to go beyond mere coincidence. It is also very interesting to note that three elderly people have died in this house, a pattern that cannot be ignored when considering the haunted happenings. More often than not, where there's one ghost, there are more, and the circumstances that keep them in that place are often related. Today, Gina's parents still live in the upper level of the house, where the scent of an old lady's perfume can still be detected. Another of Gina's brothers now occupies the ground floor. This brother admits that he occasionally sees a figure or some unexplained movement out of the corner of his eye. He has

Looking out into the downstairs hallway where Gina's husband witnessed something blocking the light. (Note her grandmother's sewing cabinet on the left.)

also heard the sounds of cabinet doors opening and closing in the kitchen, and dishes being rattled. Though unnerving, none of the activity has ever been threatening.

When Bob and I visited during the summer of 2005, I didn't encounter anything unusual, and there wasn't anything out of the ordinary on the photos or on audio. However, when we entered one room Bob felt a very strong presence (or two?) sweep over him. Only afterward did we find out that this was the room where Gina's grandparents had died.

Perhaps these are the spirits of three elderly people who died in this house, who still leave telltale signs of their presence. Do they still cling to the world of the living to watch over loved ones, or is there something about this place that prevents them from moving on? Hopefully, the pattern of death and lingering spirits will someday be broken and their souls will find peace.

Of course, no one can say for sure. Time supposedly heals all wounds, but does it heal all hauntings?

Murder Update

Sometimes it seems as if the forces of nature are working against you, but I like to look at such situations as tests of one's level of commitment. It's only fair then, that when you do go that extra mile, you are rewarded in some way. However, when that situation involves a ghost investigation at the site of a double hatchet murder on the anniversary night of the crime, those rewards can be frightening.

The pre-dawn hours of January 8, 2005, were not promising. When I let out my dogs, I found that it was sleeting and everything was coated with a thick layer of ice. I turned on the Weather Channel and saw that they were predicting several inches of snow and significant icing throughout the day.

It was very disappointing news. For several weeks I had been eagerly anticipating a return visit to the old Van Winkle house in Hawthorne, New Jersey, which is now owned by Henry Tuttman, who is restoring the place to its former splendor. The house had been the site of the gruesome murders of Judge and Mrs. Van Winkle in 1850. I wrote about the incident—and subsequent century and a half of ghostly phenomena—in *Ghost Investigator Volume 4: Ghosts of New York and New Jersey*. However, I'm never completely satisfied by simply writing about other's experiences. Nothing compares with personal encounters. I wanted to return to conduct a full investigation, and what better time than the actual night that the murderer had swung his hatchet?

Unfortunately, in addition to the weather concerns, my husband, Bob, had a nasty chest cold, and it was obvious he wouldn't be going. Mike also had a cold that he couldn't shake. I had hurt my back shoveling heavy snow and ice from a previous storm, and had seriously re-aggravated it that morning, to the point that I couldn't even bend over and pick up my bag of ghost hunting gear. Prudence would have dictated that Mike and I avoid potentially hazardous driving conditions, and just stay home and nurse our illnesses and injuries.

But it was the site of a double murder…

On the anniversary of the bloody crime…

And we really, *really*, wanted to go…

Around 10pm that night, Mike picked me up and we headed for Hawthorne, New Jersey. We arrived safe and sound, Henry gave us a tour and some updates, and we soon got down to business.

The first task was to set up camcorders and equipment in the north section of the attic where the murderer had entered the house that night, and the upstairs room where the original staircase leading down to the first floor (the path the murderer took inside the house) had been located. On the way upstairs, I switched on my digital EMF meter and noticed rather high readings on the landing of the staircase. This is the same staircase where a previous owner always felt a very strong presence. The staircase has also been the focus of attention over the years of several pets that have stared for hours at something beyond human vision.

Hurrying back downstairs for my digital camera, I quickly took a few pictures of the stairs and landing. In the second photo, there was a bright spot near the window. If you have read any of my previous books, you know I have had my suspicions about the validity of most "orbs," unless there is other supporting evidence. In this case, there was the high EMF readings, as well as the history of activity on this staircase. Also, there was an unusual occurrence with the camera that had only happened one other time—at the former mental hospital that I investigated and wrote about in *Ghost Investigator Volume 3*.

The camera had properly stored the photos, because I was able to show them to Mike. However, several minutes later, Don Smith (the author and historian who is writing a history of the house) arrived, and I attempted to show him the picture with the bright spot. The camera struggled with the file of photo #2, and finally displayed the message that the file could not be found. The other pictures were fine, but somehow something had interfered with *that* particular photo after it had been stored, and it appeared to be lost forever.

The following day, I still received the same error message that the file could not be found, but I finally did manage to resurrect some of the data. Only a horizontal slice of the original image could be retrieved, but that section just so happened to contain the bright spot by the window! Could this all have been a combination of dust, a camera error, and then a coincidence that only that section of the picture reappeared? Sure, but none of that explains the high EMF readings, which subsequently *disappeared* from the staircase.

I was only able to retrieve this slice of the photo. The bright spot is on the right of the window frame.

The house now had my complete attention. As I set up my equipment in the attic, there was an unsettling sensation knowing that I was on the spot where a murderer had broken into the house carrying a hatchet and a butcher knife exactly 154 years ago. Mike set up his equipment in the room across the hall from the attic stairs. He later explained that he felt very uncomfortable every time he went in that room.

In addition to being the site of the former staircase, there is a door on the south side of this room that marks the boundary between the original 1761 part of the house and the 1811 structure built by Judge Van Winkle. Henry told us it was impossible to keep that door closed. The latch would be secured, but when he would return the next day the door would be standing wide open. He even tried removing the door from its hinges and re-installing it to try to solve the problem.

Once all the equipment was up and running, we left the second floor so as not to disturb the sites. The next location was essential to our investigation—the kitchen, where Henry had been kind enough to put out a delicious selection of midnight snacks. Refueled, we went down into the basement. Our infrared camcorders picked up flurries of tiny specs in the air, but as there is a dirt floor, I was certain that normal particles in the air accounted for this. There were no anomalous readings, no cold spots, and no uncomfortable feelings. This may not be scientific, but for a very old house with such a grisly history, this is a surprisingly "un-creepy" basement.

Some people may be disappointed that I can't add a spooky basement story to this account, but I believe the complete lack of any paranormal activity there is an important aspect. The contrast only adds weight to the pronounced activity in other parts of house. As investigators, it is also reassuring to know that even under such circumstances we can remain objective and not let our imaginations run unchecked.

It is also important to understand that we were calm and relaxed as we entered the final phase of the investigation—the murder room. In 1850, it had been two small rooms, as a wall divided the Van Winkle's bedroom from a parlor. The wall was later removed, but a narrow floorboard among the wide planks still marks its former location.

The warmth and glow from a large fireplace in the parlor had a dual effect—it made the room quite cozy, but after I turned out the lights, I was reminded that this was very much how the room appeared to the murderer the night he crept in with his hatchet raised...

We decided the best approach to covering the room was to set up camcorders at opposite ends. Mike was in the northwest corner of the room (where the Van Winkles had been attacked), while I was in the southeast corner. At first nothing happened, and it seemed as though the spirits were resting in peace. Then we decided to ask if there was anyone who wanted to communicate, and Mike went on to speak the names of the Van Winkles and their murderer. A moment or two passed, then a tingling chill shot up my spine like a lightning bolt, and I actually shuddered from the electric effect. The feeling was overpowering, and it did not subside.

What was most bizarre—and what I did not immediately realize— was that with the onset of the chill, I had raised my right arm and was flexing my hand, alternating between outstretched fingers and a clenched fist. It was not a conscious action, and even after I realized what I was doing, I felt compelled to continue. Finally, I had to step away from the corner as the feeling grew in intensity. Mike and I changed positions, and once I was on the other side of the room, the spine-tingling sensation ceased, as did the strange action of my right arm.

Fortunate for me, but not so fortunate for Mike, who now stood in my place. He quickly had the distinct and unpleasant sensation that someone was directly behind him. I felt bad subjecting him to that corner alone, so I decided to return to where I had been standing when it all started. Almost immediately the chill swept through me again and my right arm lifted. I should explain that it did not feel as if someone was externally forcing my arm to move, it was an *internal* sensation, and an extremely compelling one. I am never thrilled by having paranormal energy evoke physical responses, but if something in that house found it easier to communicate by messing with me, I was going to let it—for a short time, at least.

The presence behind Mike (who was about three feet to my left) apparently shifted directly behind me, as we both clearly heard a sound. At first it began like a light scraping, but grew into a distinct sound of fabric tearing. I wasn't moving a muscle, and afterwards when I checked, found that none of my clothes were torn, so the sound hadn't come from me! The tearing sound had only lasted a few seconds, but it really made my skin crawl. However, that was only the beginning...

A few seconds later, there was a deep, hollow sound from above. It was faint, and sounded like it originated from the second floor, or perhaps even as far away as the attic. I likened it to the sound of striking one of those large tanks used for home heating oil—the point being it had a slight reverberation and seemed metallic. Tense moments passed in the darkness of the murder room...

Then came one of the most shocking sounds I have ever heard. It came from the northwest corner of the room, somewhere near where the Van Winkles would have been sleeping peacefully, moments before the hatchet and butcher knife were to do their awful work. It began as a soft whistling or rasping, and was so clear that at first I thought it must be something perfectly normal. Then it grew into a deep, wheezing sound, as if fluid-filled lungs were struggling to draw one last breath. Then there was an agonizingly slow exhale...then silence.

Stunned, I asked Mike if he had heard it, and he had. I actually gasped from the shock of it all, and told him that if I wasn't frozen to the spot, I probably would be running. He also said his legs were locked in place.

It's impossible to adequately describe this encounter, or how deeply it impacted us. Mrs. Van Winkle had died on the floor in a pool of her own blood within minutes of the brutal attack, and there we were 154 years later, quite possibly at the exact moment of her death, distinctly hearing what I would swear in court sounded like someone's dying breath!

Would there be more phantom breathing, or perhaps screams, or the sounds of a struggle? Would the Judge's cries of, "Murder! Murder!" echo across the centuries?

We stood there in the darkness, practically breathless, our ears straining to detect any other sounds passing across the fragile barrier between life and death. Minutes passed, the tension remained high, but there was only silence. I suggested to Mike that we take the opportunity of this lull to bring in Henry and Don, in order to have more witnesses present should anything else occur.

When Henry came in, we checked Mike's videotape to see if the "death breath," as I came to refer to it, had been captured on tape. Mike anxiously hit rewind and then play, and we all leaned toward the camcorder.

There it was! It was not as loud and distinct as we had heard, but Henry agreed it sounded like someone breathing. What was also startling was that just before the "death breath," the camcorder recorded a sharp banging noise (is if something hard or heavy struck the floor) that must have originated very close to the camcorder's microphone. We could not remember actually hearing such a sound at the time, and when I checked my videotape the next day, that banging sound had *not* been recorded by my camcorder! There is no way that a normal sound of that magnitude would not be picked up by my camcorder just twenty feet away.

My videotape did capture the "death breath," but only as a very faint whistling or hissing sound. Although I had hoped for something more distinct, in a way this was positive, as it was further proof that the sound had indeed originated on the other side of the room.

Henry and Don sat down, and the four of us waited. Don was uncomfortable, and later admitted that he had silently prayed for nothing more to happen. A short time later he left the room, and the three of us waited. And waited. Nothing. No noises, no tingling sensations, and I no longer felt compelled to raise my arm and clench my fist. The atmosphere was completely different, and as I said at the time, "It feels like an ordinary living room now."

Of course, the old Van Winkle house is anything but ordinary. That night provided one of the most dramatic and startling experiences of my ghost investigating career—and considering where I've been and what I've encountered, that is no small statement!

In the following days, I carefully reviewed the photos and video. Apart from a few white spots (which might have been dust) that passed by the camcorder in the attic, there wasn't anything else unusual. Mike and I exchanged several emails describing what we had, and had not, recorded, and I looked forward to getting copies of his tapes for a side-by-side comparison.

In addition to the tapes, Mike emailed me a sound file of a noise he recorded in the empty room across from the attic door. No one was

Mike checks his EMF meter by the fireplace in the murder room shortly before we turned out the lights and heard the "death breath."

in the room as the camcorder was running, but there was an odd and distinct rasping, grinding sound that lasted a second or two.

Mike thought it could be a voice saying, "Hello," or at least trying to speak the word. I thought it sounded more metallic or mechanical rather than a voice. In any event, it was a sound that should not have been there!

In the following weeks, I analyzed all the tapes, photos and other evidence, and sent a report to Henry. While we didn't find anything particularly threatening, there were clearly paranormal forces at work here that I hoped to someday investigate further.

That day would come in July 2005. Through another seemingly cosmic orchestration of schedules, we arranged to have psychic Cyra Greene visit the house one Friday night. Mike, his girlfriend Molly, and I arrived at the house about 8pm. Henry and I then went to the train station to pick up Cyra.

For the first hour or so, Cyra toured the house and property, getting herself oriented and getting a general feel for the place. Around 9:30pm, we were in the attic (which was rather hot on that steamy summer night!) and she said that while there was a pervading sense of fear throughout the house, it had become much stronger up here. Then something hit her (energetically, not physically).

Grabbing the right side of her head in pain, Cyra began describing making contact with a "woman's spirit" that brought heaviness to her chest and made her want to cry. She was wearing some type of old-fashioned bonnet, was attractive and intelligent, but had a look of absolute shock on her face.

She felt that this spirit was unable to "go away, can't go this way or go that way. It's just held here, dangling...it's an *awful* thing. Her soul just stopped, worse than death, stuck, can't move on. Stuck here."

Cyra explained that she felt that this was the spirit of Mrs. Van Winkle, who had been completely stunned by her own sudden and brutal murder by someone she had known and trusted. Her soul had no time to prepare for her death, and her spirit rose up from the body and just hung suspended above the site of her murder, where it has remained for over a century and a half.

"When a spirit doesn't go anywhere, it haunts," she continued. "And violent death often leads to a haunting."

As she spoke, the intense pain Cyra was experiencing began to ease and she felt that the spirit of Mrs. Van Winkle was finally beginning to get some glimmer of understanding as to what was happening. Her poor spirit had been paralyzed with fear and shock from the attack and had been in this terrible limbo all of these years. Cyra realized that our main goal was to set her lost soul into motion and liberate her from this netherworld of despair.

Cyra then felt we should go downstairs to the empty room across from the attic door. Once there, I asked her for more details about Mrs. Van Winkle. She described her high social standing, the respect she received from others, and her generous nature.

I was recording everything Cyra was saying on my new Sony digital mini CD recorder, which has amazing sound quality. There are no hisses, scratchiness and static like on conventional tape recorders (nothing for EVP-ers to enhance and misinterpret!) However, when she began to describe Mrs. Van Winkle's physical features—elongated nose, almost hawk-like eyes—there is a sharp buzzing sound on the recording, as if some strong electrical field was interfering.

This was the only time all night this interference occurred, and aside from the light fixture there were no sources of electricity in that room. Even when I was in Henry's office with the air conditioner, computers and several large printers, there was not even the slightest interference.

Was this buzzing a glitch, or was Mrs. Van Winkle acknowledging her description. (Or perhaps objecting to it!)

Although the headache had now passed completely, Cyra again mentioned how painful it had been. I reminded her that Mrs. Van Winkle had been hit in the head with a hatchet, and perhaps this "point of contact" with her spirit was more meaningful than we first thought.

I asked if there were signs of any other spirits present—Judge Van Winkle, the murderer John Johnston, or anyone else from the distant or more recent past. She did not sense anyone else, and especially felt that the Judge had sufficient time to come to grips with his imminent death and give his soul time to prepare.

A couple of days later, I mentioned this to Don Smith, who told me that the Judge indeed had time to prepare. In fact, before his death later that evening, he had the presence of mind to plan the funeral for he and his wife—even down to the details of which passages from the Bible should be read! Astonishing, considering he had literally been disemboweled in the attack.

Cyra then spent some time outside, while Henry showed us the original floor plan of the house, which had been compiled and expertly drawn before the renovations and construction in the early 1900s. It was fascinating to chart the path of the murderer through the house, through doorways that have since been moved and staircases that no longer exist. It was a chilling reminder that all of the stories and theories have a very concrete basis in reality.

When Cyra returned, we all sat quietly in the upstairs hall between the attic stairs and the empty room. Again, she had been drawn to the area above the murder scene. She further described Mrs. Van Winkle's spirit as very gray, weak, passive, unconscious. This was a haunting, but not the type that was overt or threatening, so some might not recognize it as such. This particular haunting drained energy, making one feel tired and resigned. Cyra felt that if she lived in this house she would take on these characteristics and slowly be drained of her strength.

Something had to be done, for everyone's sake.

Returning to the attic, Cyra began to speak to Mrs. Van Winkle, and asked that we all visualize sending her light and energy. Explaining that the terrible crime had been committed long ago, she urged the suspended spirit to trust us, to move beyond the fear and shock, and to move on to a place where she could be reunited with her family and friends.

It was a long, emotional process, which continued downstairs in the murder room. But in the end, Cyra began to smile.

"I think she's beginning to let go. I think she is getting the energy to move on. This is all that we can do, the rest is up to her."

Has this investigation into a double homicide committed over 150 years ago led to the release of a spirit that has been trapped in this house ever since? Has Cyra's compassion and understanding sparked a rebirth of a lost soul? It seems almost too much to hope for, yet we must hope that this is one case that has a happy ending.

There was one final curious thing that happened that night. We were all in the kitchen, and while Cyra spoke with Henry about what had transpired, Mike, Molly and I were gathered around the center island. The equipment was packed and we were just making small talk and having some refreshments. We had assumed the night's activities had come to a close, and none of us was expecting anything else unusual.

It's easiest to begin by explaining what happened from my perspective:

I was sitting at the south end of the countertop, while Mike was standing on the side to my right (probably no more than two feet away), and Molly was sitting immediately to his right. Suddenly, something directly in front of me caught my attention. For a split second I thought it was a white moth, because it was about an inch in diameter, and was bright white. But then I saw it was more of a light than a solid object and it passed directly in front of me about one foot above the countertop, moving from right to left.

There was a container on the counter just a little farther than arm's reach, and I watched as the small white light moved very rapidly in front of the container, giving me the ability to determine just how close it had been. It was visible for perhaps a yard off to my left before it vanished.

Before I could speak and ask if anyone else had seen the bizarre light, something of the same size, intensity and proximity sped by on the same level course, also disappearing after several feet. I am not ashamed to say that my initial unscientific assessment was, *That was no ******* moth!*

Pausing just a second to see if it would happen a third time, I then immediately looked to Mike and saw that he was looking behind him, and then he turned to look at the countertop, and then looked behind him again. I glanced at Molly and she was looking back and forth between Mike and I, and we all had a similar expression of surprise. Finally overcoming our few seconds of being stunned into speechlessness, we all spoke at the same time.

"Did you see that?"

"What did you see?"

"What was that?"

"Did you hear what I just heard?"

There were another few moments of confusion, and then we hashed it all out:

An instant before I saw the first light zip in front of me, Mike saw it pass between us and turned to see if it was some kind of light coming through the window. As he was realizing that the light was inside the kitchen, not coming from any outside source, the second light raced past him, just inches away.

Molly was not able to corroborate our story, as she did not see anything. However, she had *heard* something—something she described as sounding like a baby crying right by the window. This was even stranger, as we were within a few feet of one another and yet Mike and I heard nothing.

Why was the cry of a baby heard only by Molly, followed by a pair of strange white lights seen only by Mike and I? And why didn't Cyra or Henry experience any of it? I certainly wish I had some type of explanation, but I have no clue beyond simply assuming that something was still present and trying to get our attention. Even as I write about it weeks after it occurred, I marvel at the bizarre nature of the event, and how we were affected by it.

At the very end of our late night's work, there was some talk about returning again next January on the murder anniversary night. Perhaps there are different forces at work then; perhaps all the spirits involved in the crime return to relive the horrible event that changed and ended so many lives.

If we do return, perhaps the spirits will have moved on and we will find nothing. Then again, we might just catch another breath…

Cyra sketched this portrait of Mrs. Van Winkle. She had seen her image as all gray, with the spirit's hand just hanging limply, as well as the entire figure being suspended in the air.

If at First You're Not Believed...

On Halloween in 2004, I gave a ghost lecture at the library in New City, New York. Afterward, local resident Karen Franlese spoke to me about a house where she used to live in Pomona, New York. Just a few minutes into the conversation, I knew that this was exactly the type of story for which I look, and I told her I would call when I started working on the new ghost book. As it turned out, we arranged to speak on the morning on January 9, 2005, just hours after returning from the Van Winkle house in Hawthorne, New Jersey (see page 30). I was a little punchy from lack of sleep and the excitement of the investigation, but Karen's great story kept me riveted.

Like many people in the 1960s, Karen's family moved from New York City to Rockland County. They first lived in Spring Valley, but in 1967 they moved to a house in Pomona. The place had once been a restaurant and inn, called the Swiss Alp Club, and there was a large main building and two small cottages on the property. There were stories that members of the German Bund—the American version of the Nazi party—began the private club in the 1930s and were still occupying the premises during WWII, until government authorities removed them. The house itself was built around 1910, but no early history of the occupants is known.

The family consisted of Karen, who was twenty-two, her five-year-old brother, her father, who was often away on business, and her mother, who was an antiques dealer. She also had an older sister who was married and lived elsewhere at the time. On moving day, Karen and her little brother chose their bedrooms, and then the terror began...

Every night her brother woke up screaming. He had never had any problems sleeping before, but he refused to talk about what was frightening him. It reached the point where he was terrified of going into his room, and only after falling asleep on the couch were they able to pick him up and put him to bed. Yet the screaming continued.

Karen had to get up early every morning to go to work, and she complained to her mother that something had to be done about the situation so she could get some sleep. As her brother still wouldn't tell them what was wrong, Karen suggested they switch bedrooms and see if that alleviated the situation. The move was a mixed blessing.

The Franlese family still has the original sign from the place that may have been a front for the Nazi party.

While her brother was very happy in his new room, and never again woke up screaming, Karen's troubles were just beginning. The very first night in her brother's old room, she felt as if she was "walking into a tomb." Sounds seemed oddly muffled, and the atmosphere was very heavy, uncomfortable and somewhat disorienting. Her mother dismissed her daughter's feelings by simply saying, "Oh, it's just an old house," as if that explained everything.

Karen managed to get to sleep, but in the middle of the night someone knocked loudly on the front door. Her room was the first room to the right by the door, so she dragged herself out of bed to see who the late night visitor could be. No one was there. It seemed odd that someone would be playing a prank at that time of night, especially considering that the house was rather secluded.

However, every night the knocking continued, and every night Karen got up to see if anyone was there. Her mother claimed that she didn't hear the knocking, but she could hear Karen getting up and opening the front door.

A family snapshot of the house from 1967.

"Why do you keep opening the door in the middle of the night?" her mother demanded to know.

"Because someone keeps knocking!" Karen countered in her defense.

Somewhat annoyed, her mother explained that the house was over five hundred feet from the road, and if anyone had driven up she would have heard the car. Therefore, no one could be knocking on the front door. Despite her mother's weak attempt at logic, the knocking continued, but Karen kept getting so much grief from her mother that she stopped trying to see who was there.

However, even if she had been capable of completely ignoring the phantom knocking, she couldn't shut out the sounds of footsteps in the hall at night. It was a long hallway, and clear, male footsteps could be heard going down the length of the house every night.

"But I didn't say anything to my mother about the footsteps, because I had been yelled at enough," Karen said, frustrated that her own mother had not believed her.

44

Of course, it isn't easy coming to grips with the fact that your home is haunted, and often the simplest way to deal with the situation is to go into denial.

At least Karen had one member of the household who was on her side—the family pet, a large German Shepherd. The dog would often stare intently at blank space, or a section of a wall, and his eyes would follow something no one else could see. He would become very agitated and bark as if trying to protect the family. One night, Karen said, "Okay, that's it, this dog is seeing something!"

"It's just shadows," her mother replied in her usual dismissive manner.

In a way, she was most probably right this time—only it was shadows of the dead that the dog was most likely seeing.

This dog was a "witness" to another strange event. All of the family members often heard footsteps coming up the basement stairs. One day when Karen's mother was alone in the house with the dog, the footsteps began again, and they were so loud she was sure it must be someone who had broken into the house. The dog heard the intruder as well, and ran to the basement door, listening and staring intently. This was not casual curiosity on the dog's part, as all the hair was standing up on his back.

The mother also waited in fear by the door, and was breathless as the footsteps stopped on the top step. She and the dog waited to see if the intruder would try to open the door. They waited, and waited, and finally she found the courage to pull open the door and confront the man who had broken into her home. No one was there.

The footsteps had clearly ended at the top step, and she hadn't heard the person go back down the stairs. A search of the basement revealed no one, and no signs of forced entry. Yet without a doubt someone had just climbed those stairs. Even if she had been imagining it, surely the German Shepherd was not delusional. However, did this incident convince the mother that the house was haunted? Not that she would openly admit!

She would not even relent when a stranger came to the house and made a surprising statement. In the course of her antiques business, other dealers would often come to the house to purchase items for their stores. One day her mother opened the front door to let in a dealer and he immediately walked straight into Karen's room. He had never before been in the house, but he took one look at the mirror in her room and calmly stated, "You know you have a ghost here."

Karen's mother was startled, and didn't know how to respond. The man continued with his remarkable statement.

"He is a good ghost, though. He won't cause any problems. I would have seen red if he was evil."

Now, most people would have questioned the man to find out exactly what he saw. However, even though everyone heard footsteps, and both her son and daughter had bizarre experiences in the very room the dealer had zeroed in on, the mother didn't ask any further questions! Denial is a remarkable thing...

The most startling encounter came one night in 1973. Karen had plans to be married, and would soon be moving out of the house. Perhaps the entity that walks the halls of this house realized that she would be leaving, and decided to make her farewell a memorable one.

Karen woke up in the middle of night and saw a bright light at the foot of her bed. At first, she thought it was just a light, but then she saw a figure of man amidst the bright glow. Not taking her eyes off the figure, she reached over to the nightstand and grabbed her glasses. The man obligingly remained so she could get a clear look at him.

He was blond, with vibrant blue eyes. He was wearing a brown robe. Most intriguing, he was carrying a tray that was covered with little bottles of all shapes and sizes. The figure appeared to be so real and so solid, that Karen believed that she was looking at a real living human being.

Then it hit her—the bright light, the odd appearance of this man...

Oh my God! This has to be the ghost! Karen suddenly realized.

The instant that thought came into her head, the man began to fade from sight and quickly disappeared.

"Then I got mad," Karen recalled. "I said all these years you've kept me awake, and when you finally appear you just fade away when I realize who you are!"

Although the encounter with the blond, blue-eyed ghost was the most remarkable thing she ever saw, Karen chose not to tell her mother about it. She knew what her mother's reaction would be, and decided not to waste her breath.

However, there is a devilishly delightful saying that what goes around, comes around...

Soon after Karen moved out, her mother decided that she had put up with her husband's snoring long enough. She decided to sleep in her daughter's old room. It was payback time...

Just a few days later, Karen's mother called her and asked, "What is it about that room?"

"Ma, I don't know what you're talking about," Karen replied playing dumb, milking the situation with great satisfaction.

"There's such an eerie feeling in there," her mother continued, as if she had made some new discovery. "It's like being in another world! And someone keeps knocking on the front door, and there's footsteps down the hall every night!"

Karen finally explained that those were exactly the same phenomena she had endured night after night. Then she couldn't resist reminding her mother how much grief she had given her about these very things for six years. It was so satisfying to finally be believed!

In the years following, Karen's father died, and her mother decided to sell the place in 1983. One day Karen was there when prospective buyers were coming over, and her mother warned her, "Do not say *anything* about a ghost!" Apparently, however, no one needed to tell the next owner that his new home was haunted.

An actor bought the property, and one day he called Karen and asked how he could "find out about the house."

"I played dumb," Karen explained. "I asked him what he meant. He said he wanted to find out about certain 'happenings' in the house."

Karen decided not to share the stories of her ghostly encounters, and the new owner did not elaborate on his "happenings" either. She subsequently did hear that there was a lot trouble at the house, but not of the paranormal variety—police were often called in on domestic situations, and there were rumors of other illegal activity. After that owner died, Karen lost track of the house and its occupants.

While Karen was very clear and thorough with her accounts, there was one subject about which I needed to question her further—the blond, blue-eyed man with a tray who appeared at the foot of her bed. Someone had suggested to her that since the place had been a restaurant, he might be the spirit of a former waiter. However, I have yet to see any waiter wearing a long brown robe.

"What was your impression at the time? Who do you think he was?" I asked.

"It looked like he was wearing a monkish-type robe," she replied after a moment of thought. "He did give me the impression that he was something like a Benedictine monk."

"And the bottles," I continued. "What did you feel was in those bottles?"

"They were small, like the size of airline liquor bottles, but some were square, some were round. I guess I thought they were full of medicines."

At this point, there is no documented evidence that would place monks on this property, but ghosts can arrive from many paranormal avenues. Had some healing man of the cloth died near this spot as he traveled, practicing his art in some distant time in the past? Could some antique item that was brought into the house also have brought his spirit? Had this Aryan-looking man somehow been connected to the Germans who once occupied this place?

More importantly, the questions of the present and future still remain. Are the current owners experiencing the same haunted activity?

I had strongly considered writing a letter to "Whom it May Concern" or "Current Occupant" to ask if they felt there were ghosts in their house. However, if nothing unusual was happening I did not want to plant the seed of fear.

Peace of mind is a precious and scarce commodity. After all, it's not like you can find it even in an entire tray of medicines...

Window to the Other World

In the Hudson Valley region there are some common misconceptions homeowners have about their houses and property. I wish I had a dollar for each person who believes that his house was built on an old Indian burial ground. Then there are the owners who insist that Revolutionary War soldiers camped on their property. For those who have an old house with a hidden room or secret passage, it's almost unanimously believed that this must mean the house was a stop on the underground railroad. Then there are the rumors of witches, cults, suicides, murders and bodies buried in the basement.

While all of these scenarios may make for good stories, few places can muster the hard evidence to back up these claims. It is rare that documentation exists, and rarer still when actual artifacts are discovered. So, when Larry Chapman began telling me about a haunted house where he used live in Montgomery, New York, where he had uncovered dozens of artifacts from Native Americans and Revolutionary War soldiers, I didn't want to waste any time arranging an investigation. Fortunately his nephew, Brian Miller, is the current owner, and I called him and arranged to come by that same week.

The original stone house was built in the 1700s. This structure has been referred to as a fort, and while it may not have been a regular army installation, it was most likely designed with defense in mind. Other such buildings in Orange County provided refuge for the local populace in times of danger, and it's easy to imagine farmers and their families fleeing to the safety of the stone walls when trouble was brewing with Indians in the area.

While there are no known records of actual conflicts with Native Americans at this particular location, there is little doubt that this land was once inhabited by them. Larry has uncovered dozens of arrowheads, an impressive stone ax head and a fascinating grinding stone. And yes, there are rumors of a burial ground on the property behind the house. In this case, as there is clear evidence of an Indian settlement, it would actually make sense that they would have buried their dead somewhere nearby.

It is also believed that American soldiers during the Revolutionary War used the structure as something of a fort (or a least a

These arrowheads, grinding stone and ax heads are just some of the Native American artifacts Larry Chapman has discovered on the property.

headquarters), and camped on the property. It is even thought that George Washington spent some time here. Larry and other family members have uncovered many period items from the dirt of the basement and the surrounding grounds consistent with a military presence. Among the many finds have been pieces of weapons, buckles, a cannon ball, and other Revolutionary War era items that would have

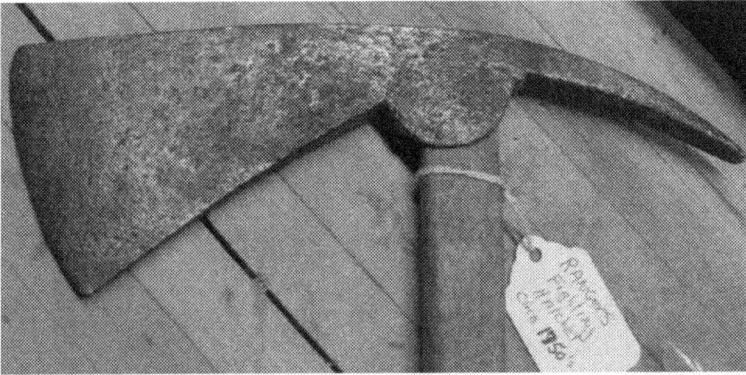

A hatchet Larry found, which has been identified as the type used by American Rangers during the Revolutionary War. (The handle is not original.)

been used by American soldiers. Hopefully, further research will be able to identify which group of soldiers occupied the site, and for how long they were camped at this location.

Larry has also found Civil War era military artifacts, which suggest that perhaps some local regiment may have temporarily stayed at this location before heading off to war.

Of course, just because Indians may have lived and died on a certain piece of property, and wounded and sick soldiers may also have passed there, it doesn't mean that the place must have ghosts. However, death is the only essential ingredient for a haunting, and a haunting appears to be the prime suspect for the bizarre activities that have occurred in this house over the years. And it all began in a very curious manner...

Generally, ghosts come to a house, but in this case, the house actually came to the ghosts. The current structure was built in the late 1930s by Larry's parents. It was situated near Orange County Airport, but in the early 1940s the airport was to undergo an expansion. The house would either have to be demolished or relocated, and as there was no reason to spoil a relatively new building, the family decided to pick it up and move it. As they owned large tracts of land in the area, the only question was where to put their temporarily mobile home.

Unfortunately for the old stone house, it had been abandoned and fell into disrepair in the late 1800s. Many of the stones used to construct its walls were carted away to build a nearby farmhouse.

A postcard from the early 20th century showing the ruins of the stone house. The caption reads, "Ruins of a Revolutionary Dwelling used as a camp by Soldiers in 1776, Kaisertown, Montgomery, N.Y."

An earlier photo depicting the rear of the structure's deteriorating condition. (Courtesy of Larry Chapman.)

However, its foundation was still intact, and it turned out to be just the right size. Utilizing some massive wooden beams from another structure (some have speculated that they may have come from a ship), the old foundation was prepared to receive the new house. In retrospect, of course, it may have been worth the effort to build a new foundation somewhere else, but how could the family know what they were getting themselves into? In 1944, the house was transported to its historic, and haunted, location.

The new house was placed on the old foundation in 1944. Note the large beams on the lawn. (Courtesy of Larry Chapman.)

While Larry's mother lived in the house for many years, she never spoke about ghosts. She was reputedly very "closed-mouth" about such matters, and it isn't surprising that she would not have mentioned any strange happenings. As a result, it isn't clear how soon after the house was placed on the old stone foundation that unexplained events began to occur. Other family members admittedly did experience paranormal activity early on, but as their experiences were not recorded and they have all since passed away, we can only look to the recent past with any certainty.

In 2001, Larry's mother had a stroke. The house was in need of repair, so while she was in the hospital Larry decided to work on some renovations. He lived in the house next door, so it was convenient to spend time on his mother's house after work every day. One of the first odd things he noticed was that tools he left in one room at the end of the evening would be in another part of the house when he returned the next day. Naturally, everyone misplaces things, but these moving tools become so obvious and so routine that he learned to accept and live with the invisible prankster. Also, he kept finding old books stacked on the attic stairs. He would remove them, but the next day he would find more books on the stairs. While it was clear he was not alone in the house, he never actually felt afraid. But that was to change, in a big way…

Larry was working on the kitchen floor when the footsteps began. They were loud, heavy footsteps, as if a large man wearing boots was making his way up the staircase from the basement. The door to the basement was just off the kitchen, and to Larry's amazement, the footsteps did not cease when they came to the closed door. As if there was no door at all, the sounds of the "intruder" continued uninterrupted across the kitchen floor—although no one was visible!

Passing through the kitchen with an icy cold blast of air, the phantom boots then pounded their way into the living room, and turned right into another room. In the corner of this room were the stairs to the attic, and the ghostly inhabitant then proceeded up that staircase. Only when it had reached the attic did the footsteps stop, and the house was once again silent.

Night after the night the same routine played out—the heavy footsteps up the basement stairs, through the kitchen (usually passing right behind Larry's back, making his hair stand up on end), then up to the attic. As unnerving as it was during the first encounter, each successive visitation became harder and harder to bear. Finally, Larry's nerves could take no more.

Grabbing a claw hammer, Larry swung at the phantom walker as it passed through the kitchen. He also shouted curses at the restless spirit, threatened it, and yelled, "Come on, come and get me!" The action was futile as the hammer swung through empty space, but he had been pushed to the limit, and instinctively tried to strike back at the thing that had been frightening him.

While Larry's reaction was perfectly understandable, it probably wasn't the wisest thing he could have done…

Several days later, Larry was working in the attic. While there was an uncomfortable feeling, he was at least spared the sounds of the footsteps. Had he chased away the spirit? Had he made it clear that this was his house, and no ghosts were welcome?

Well, not exactly.

As Larry began descending the attic stairs, something shoved him from behind with such force that he was thrown forward into the wall above the doorway. He described the impact as feeling as though he had been hit in the back by a car. Had he simply tripped, he would have fallen straight down the stairs, but his feet did not touch the stairs as he went forward through the air. Again, if he had only tripped, even if his arms had been outstretched, he would not have been able to touch the wall so high up.

When the force propelled him into the wall, his hands reached out for anything for which to grab hold. His mother had put several nails above the doorway to hang up various items, and these nails cut into Larry's hands as he struggled to hang on. But whatever force had pushed him through the air, did not continue to hold him up, and he fell onto the stairs below. Dazed, scared and bleeding, he realized that threatening the invisible entity with a hammer must have angered the spirit and provoked it to violence. He was not going to make the same mistake twice.

While no physical harm would come to him again, strange things continued to happen. One day his wife was in the house and clearly heard someone in the basement. Assuming it was Larry, she called down to him from the doorway. When there was no response, she yelled at him to cut it out and come upstairs. There was only silence, and when she checked the basement no one was there. Running outside, she found that Larry hadn't been anywhere near the house. (Several years later, this same scenario would be played out with Brian's mother, who heard footsteps and sounds in the basement and called down to him, but he was out in the yard.)

While there is a lot of activity in this basement, it doesn't all appear to be of human origin. One winter's evening when Larry was plowing the driveway with his tractor, the tractor lights shined through the basement windows and he thought he saw something move inside. On his next pass, the lights again illuminated the interior of the basement and he saw a large, dark, winged animal moving slowly through the air. If it was a bat, it was one enormous bat. If it was a bird, he couldn't imagine how it had gotten trapped in the basement.

When he was finished plowing, he went into the basement to find the mysterious animal. He searched high and low, around every beam and rafter, but he couldn't find any living creature, and there were absolutely no signs that anything was living down there.

On other occasions when Larry was working outside and the house was supposed to be empty, he would see a figure standing in the window watching him. Sometimes the figure appeared to be a woman, but he couldn't always tell, depending upon how far away he was. He only knew that someone was keeping an eye on him.

This inexplicable activity may have spilled over into Larry's house, which is built on the site of the old wagon barn. His basement is something of a museum of items he has both found and purchased,

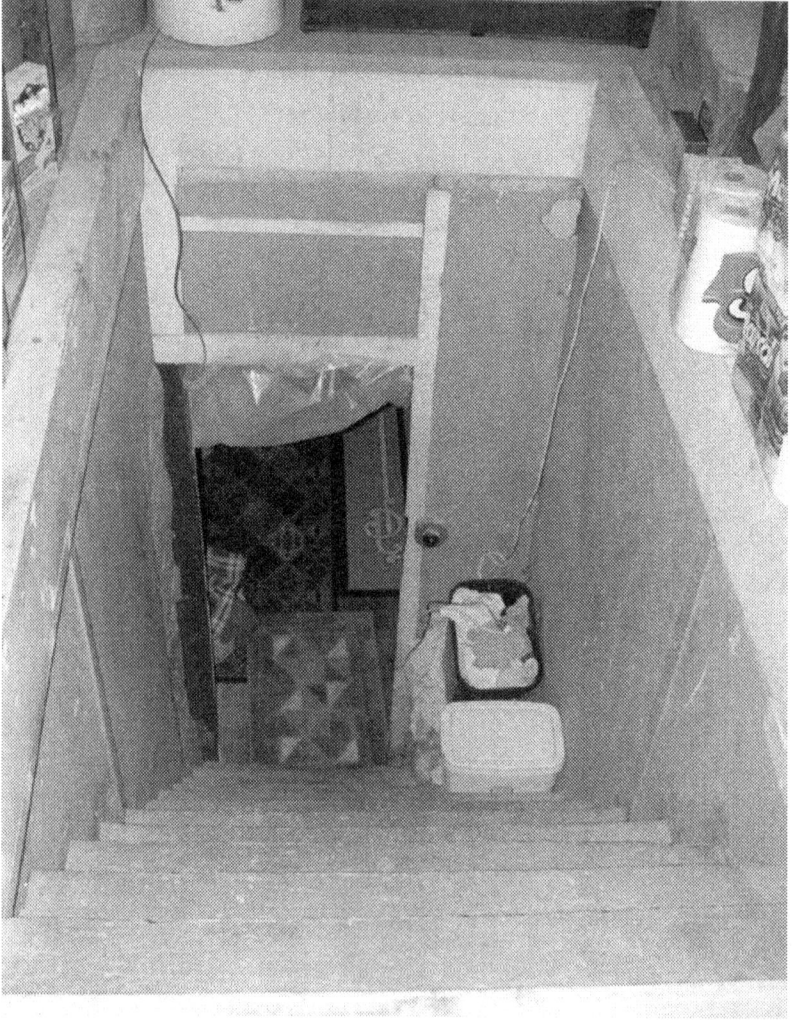

The attic staircase. Larry was thrown from the top of the stairs into the wall above the doorway.

from old coins, to tin litho toys, to delicate glassware. And of course, if the vindictive spirit had followed him home, which items would it choose to throw?

On many occasions over the past few years, both Larry and his wife would hear unusual noises in the basement, followed by a smashing sound. They would go downstairs and find that something had been knocked off a shelf and was lying broken on the floor. They wouldn't always hear the damage being done, however. Sometimes they would just go into the basement and find something smashed. If there is some natural explanation for these falling objects, why then does it only happen to items that are breakable? And what natural force could also explain how the radio in this basement is able to turn itself on?

Perhaps this is not the same spirit that walks the staircases of the original house, but it does appear to be equally peeved at Larry. However, he can't be responsible for the activity that occurs in the neighbor's house next door on the south side of the original structure. Built on the foundation of the carriage house, this place also has inexplicable phenomena such as lights turning on and off by themselves. It appears to be a triple haunting—three houses built on the sites of three structures that were all part of the same property, and all of the owners subjected to various degrees of paranormal activity. Hopefully no one has plans of putting a housing development anywhere nearby!

Larry's mother eventually came home from the hospital, but sadly one Monday morning the family found that she had passed away in the house in which she had lived for almost sixty years. It was finally time for a new owner, but the house would remain in the family as Larry's nephew, Brian, bought it. Growing up, Brian had heard the family's stories of things that went bump in the night, but his reaction to all the supposed ghostly happenings was a decidedly unimpressed "Yeah, right" attitude. He assumed that his uncles made up these stories to frighten the nieces and nephews, and he entered his new home ownership as a confirmed skeptic.

However, that attitude would be turned 180 degrees soon after Brian began gutting the house in the initial phases of a total restoration.

Brian was alone in the house, or so he thought. He was in his bedroom taking a nap when something woke him up. Someone was close, someone was touching him—then suddenly a pair of hands had a hold of his ankle and began tugging on his leg! He couldn't see anyone, but the hands were pulling hard—then just as suddenly they let go. Nothing else happened, and this bizarre phenomenon was never repeated, but making physical contact with an invisible entity was enough to convince Brian that his uncles hadn't been pulling his leg all those years!

Unfortunately, there was to be another startling physical incident, and it would be uncomfortably similar to what his uncle had experienced on the attic stairs. Brian was working in the basement and his thoughts were concentrated on his work. Nothing strange was going on and he didn't sense anything menacing. However, as he started to go up the stairs, something shoved him from behind, propelling him upward and to the side, right into the wall. Brian's body hit the wall with such force that it broke the drywall and left a large "impact crater." He hasn't yet replaced that section of wall, and today the damage remains as a constant reminder that in this house, you always have to watch your back.

Fortunately, not all of the activity Brian has experienced has been so threatening, but it is nonetheless upsetting. On several occasions a horrible smell has manifested in the kitchen—a smell that can only be described as rotting flesh. The first time it happened, Brian searched for a natural explanation, such as spoiled meat in the refrigerator. He couldn't find any source for the smell, and then realized that the terrible odor did not permeate the entire kitchen, just one spot near the center of the room. If you moved a step or two the stench was gone, but move back to that isolated spot and there it was again.

This rotten meat smell would disappear as quickly as it came, but the mysterious odor has reappeared several other times over the past two years. It is always at the same spot, and always smells just as bad as the first time.

Another mysterious spot in the house is literally just that—a spot on the floor of the living room. The darkened patch first appeared one Monday morning, and it seemed almost to spell out the letters "LC" (Larry's initials), or possibly "IC" (Larry's mother's initials). Several family members witnessed the spot and came to the same conclusion. Were they simply seeing shapes familiar to them, like seeing animals in clouds? Was it simply a coincidence that the dark patch appeared on a Monday, the day Larry's mother died?

Brian used his belt sander to try to remove the strange discoloration, but the stain is too deep into the wood. The area

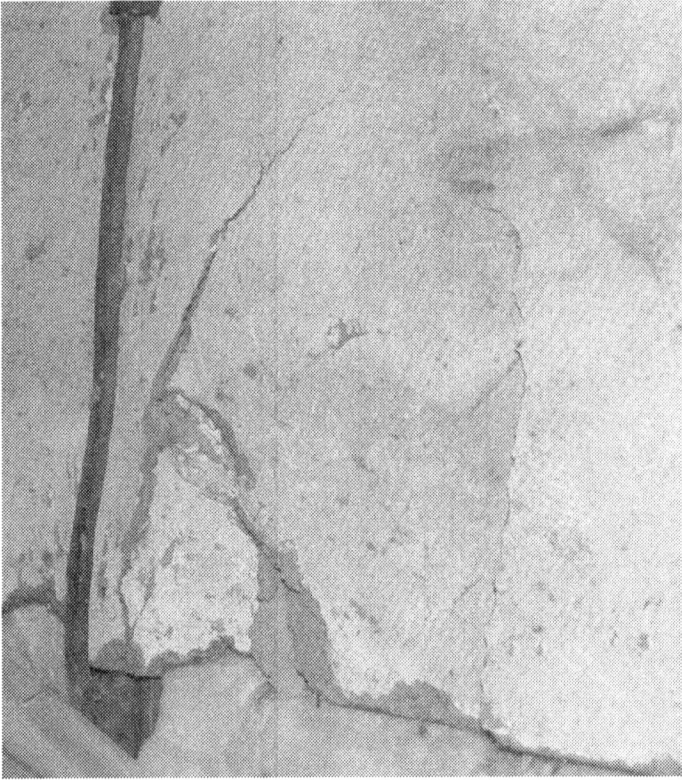

The section of drywall that was broken when Brian was shoved on the basement stairs.

eventually faded on its own, but has returned several times—and each time on a Monday! Other than that bizarre aspect, there does not seem to be any predictable pattern, such as unusually humid days, heat, cold, etc.

One day when Brian was sitting in the living room, he saw a long wisp of smoke rise up from the floor near the wall. At first he thought the house was on fire, even though he couldn't smell any smoke. He watched for a moment as the smoke rose up to the ceiling, then moved to the right across the room about twenty feet until it stopped above the strange dark patch on the floor. The smoke then dissipated.

Even with the odd behavior of the smoke, Brian thought it must be the start of an electrical fire, as the wispy trail appeared to be originating near an outlet in the wall. However, the wiring throughout the house was new, and he couldn't find any signs of a fire. Also, electrical fires produce a very distinctive acrid odor, yet this particular smoke had no scent. In addition, all of the outlets worked properly, and there has never been any more of this unique "smoke."

Brian told his family members about these strange happenings, and several of them decided to take matters into their own hands. They would conduct a type of exorcism in an attempt to send the unhappy spirit, or spirits, out of the house and on to a better place.

Nothing much happened during the proceedings, until they gathered in the kitchen and began saying the Lord's Prayer. The room grew icy cold. Then a plumb bob (a weight suspended on a cord used to mark straight lines) hanging near the wall slowly started to rotate. The weight picked up speed, then it stopped and started rotating in the opposite direction! This continued for several minutes and was witnessed by everyone present, and it was a wonder that no one ran out of the house.

Although, that may not be entirely true…

After the exorcism ceremony was complete, Brian's cousin looked out of the attic window and saw a man in the driveway. He was looking back over his shoulder at the house as he hobbled away toward the road. From what she could see from her vantage point, the man was limping because either his left leg was missing and he was using a wooden stick as a crutch, or he had a wooden leg. Then he simply vanished.

Was this the spirit that had been walking up the stairs, pushing people, smashing objects and generally making a nuisance of himself? Had he been a soldier who had his leg amputated in this house? Had the exorcism actually worked, driving away the force behind all of the bizarre activity?

Possibly, yes. While there are still some strange sounds, since that day there hasn't been any shoving, heavy footsteps or bad odors. If the spirit or spirits have not left, they have at least been relatively quiet.

As I drove to the house one April evening, I wasn't sure what we might find, if anything. But even if all the ghosts had left the building, it was important to see the place firsthand so I could better relate the stories Larry and Brian had told me. Mike Worden was joining me for the investigation, and as I navigated the unfamiliar back roads I saw Mike's car in my rearview mirror. At least if I was going to get lost, I wouldn't be alone.

The view of the driveway from the attic window where a man was seen limping toward the road.

Fortunately, Brian had given excellent directions and Mike and I pulled into the same driveway that may have been the exit point of one very unhappy, crippled spirit. While there was still daylight, Brian gave us a tour of the outside of the house, where the boundary between the old stone foundation and 60-year-old cinder block addition could be clearly seen. I recently heard a theory that rocks could possibly hold sound vibrations, like a storage device that might someday yield its historic recordings if we can develop the technology to tap into them. It's all rather far-fetched, but I couldn't help putting my hand against the foundation and thinking, *If only these walls could talk…*

After a quick tour inside, we decided to set up the equipment in the basement and the attic. One of the advantages of working with Mike is that we can set up a pair of identical cameras and instruments and record simultaneously. (A technique that proved to be very useful in the Van Winkle house. See page 30) I took the basement, while

Mike took the attic. From an investigative standpoint, it's usually best to remove yourself from the scene for a while to eliminate the chance of creating any sounds that might be misinterpreted later, so we decided to go next door and visit Larry.

Before we left, however, I wanted to check out this mysterious stain on the floor. It was clearly some kind of discoloration, but not until Brian applied a damp mop did the true extent of the stain develop. It was hard to tell what might have caused it, but it did have some distinct borders, and could be interpreted as letters. Obviously, we put water on the stain to make it stand out, but both Brian and his mother assured us that the dark patterns will suddenly appear regardless of whether it's humid or dry. We also examined the area directly under the stain in the basement, and found that there are no pipes or wires or anything that could prompt a change in the floor above.

While it was interesting, it certainly wasn't proof of anything paranormal. Then Mike suggested aiming the thermometer at the spot. It read five degrees cooler than the surrounding area, which could have been the result of the water evaporating. Brian suggested wetting another spot on the floor nearby and seeing if we got a similar cooling effect. The new wet spot continued to register 70 degrees, along with the rest of floor—except for the area of the stain. That remained a constant five or six degrees lower.

Even an hour later after everything had dried, the rest of the floor measured 70 degrees, including the portion of the floor that was not stained, but had been dampened. This time, however, the area of the stain was now eight degrees cooler! We couldn't find any logical explanation why the temperature in that small area should be so significantly less than the temperature just an inch or two away. Clearly, more was going on with this stain than met the eye...

We also took a look at Brian's bedroom, where some unseen entity had tugged on his leg. Earlier that evening he told me about the image of the crippled man who might have been missing his left leg, and I asked him if he could recall which leg was pulled. He thought for a moment and pointed toward the wall.

"It was the leg closest to the wall," he recalled, "so that would have been my left leg. Why, does that have any significance?"

I told him there was no way to be sure, but it was certainly interesting to consider that a spirit missing his left leg was possibly trying to acquire a new one!

Then we spent some time in Larry's basement, marveling over the many fascinating items he has found with his metal detector. Who doesn't get a thrill out of the prospect of uncovering buried treasure, and when this treasure also has historical significance, and may somehow be related to a haunting, it makes the finds even more exciting. Larry also joked that he could get a hammer and reenact the scene for us where he threatened the spirit, but we decided not to stir up anything negative if we could help it.

When we returned to Brian's house, we shut down all of the equipment and started packing up. Except for the temperature discrepancies on the stained area of the floor, we hadn't observed anything unusual. I told Brian I would have to review all the photos and videotapes, and would let him know if I found anything.

A few days later, I went over the photos and found something strange on one taken of the inside of the basement wall. It wasn't one of those typical white fuzzy orbs caused by dust particles, it was an irregular patch of reddish light. I carefully went over all the other basement photos, but the patch of light only appeared in this one. Also, this photo was taken without the flash, so it was not some type of reflection.

Then began the usually tedious task of reviewing all of the videotape. I began with the basement and had to take frequent breaks to avoid being lulled into a stupor by staring at an image that didn't change. Or so I thought.

About half an hour into the tape, there was a bright light moving in the upper left portion of the frame. My heart beat a little faster as I stopped the camcorder, backed up the tape a minute and played it again. It wasn't my imagination, there was a bright point of light that moved several inches and then was gone.

First rule of ghost hunting: Look for a rational explanation. The camcorder had been pointed toward the staircase, and I remembered that there was a window in the foundation to the left of the stairs. I reasoned that it most likely had simply been car headlights or taillights passing down the road.

Somewhat disappointed that the phantom light could have been a Chevy, I resumed the tape. Two minutes lately there was a loud, "Bark! Bark!"

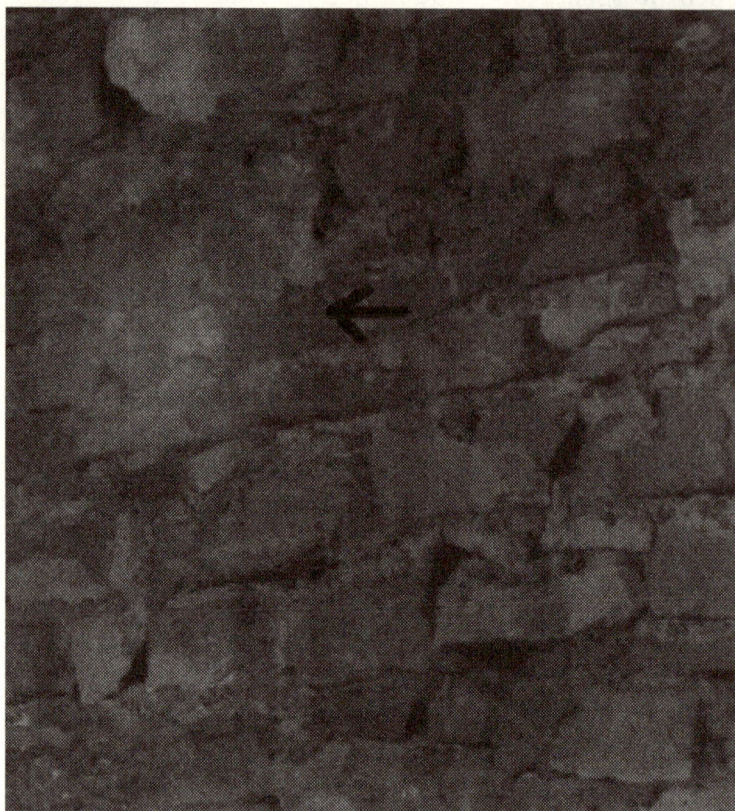

The arrow points to the patch of reddish light on the basement wall.

I knew that neither Brian nor Larry had a dog, so I assumed a neighbor's dog had wandered onto the property, as the two short barks were very close.

Great, now I've recorded a Chevy and a dog, how much more exciting can it get? I thought as I resumed the videotape once again.

About twenty seconds later, a pair of lights appeared in the window. Were these eyes? Were these the eyes of the barking dog? If so, why on earth was it looking into a dark basement window? We had made these tapes in infrared, which can "see" in complete darkness, and had turned off all the lights. Also, the infrared light, which is invisible to the human eye, and supposedly animal eyes as well, has an effective range of only about fifteen feet. If this was an animal looking in, the infrared light should not have been strong enough to reflect back from its eyes.

The pair of eye-like lights returned again as if searching for something in the basement, and just as suddenly were gone again. Three more times over the span of the next sixteen minutes there were single and double lights. The more I viewed them, the less they appeared to be characteristic of a car or an animal. But what else could they be?

When I began reviewing the attic videotape, I quickly discovered that this camcorder's microphone could pick up sounds from the road. It clearly recorded the traffic that had passed by throughout the hour, and there were far more cars than I had anticipated. Often several cars would pass within seconds, and rarely would more than a few minutes pass without a car going by.

There went my car headlight/taillight theory to account for the lights recorded out of the basement window. If you could see car lights from the road from that window, then there should have been many more recorded throughout the tape. Not one could be seen on the basement tape for the first half hour, despite the fact that many cars passed in that time. And many more cars passed in the second half hour than the seven or eight lights recorded.

Also, the attic camcorder caught the sound of the barking dog on tape. The sound was much louder in the attic, and it almost sounded as though the dog was in the house. There were several other knocking or creaking sounds, but in an old house those are to be expected so I couldn't attribute them to anything unusual on a first investigation, and without being present at the time.

Though puzzled by the lights, I still clung to some belief that the traffic on the road was somehow responsible. The eye-like lights were a little trickier, but I thought it could be the neighbor's dog or some other animal fascinated with that basement window for some bizarre reason. I thought the only unusual evidence I had was the photo of the reddish light in the basement.

A few days later, I saw Larry at a local flea market selling a few of the many items from his collection. He asked what I had found and I said, "I don't think we found too much."

I told him about the basement photo. Then I told him about the moving lights and asked, "Can you see car headlights from that basement window by the stairs?"

"No, you can't see cars from that window," he replied, much to my amazement.

He went on to explain that the window was very small and at ground level, and partially covered by dirt. From the angle of my camcorder and the position of the road, it would have been impossible to see car lights.

"Okay…" I said, processing this new information, "What about your neighbor's dog?"

"None of our neighbors have a dog," he replied.

In fact, he couldn't recall ever seeing a dog on the property.

Okay…

The next day I called Brian, and he confirmed that it would have been impossible for my camcorder to see any car lights from that basement window. In fact, there was a bucket outside in front of the window, so not only would it have blocked lights, it would have blocked any animal from looking in. He also confirmed that there were no dogs in the neighborhood.

He then relayed to me some interesting information about that particular corner of the basement. On several occasions when he was installing some pipes in that area, he heard strange and unnerving sounds, many of which sounded animal-like. He thought that Larry was outside of the window making the sounds to scare him. A few times he ran out to catch his mischievous uncle in the act, only to find no one in sight. He also found that on those occasions his uncle was at home and had not been outside for hours.

This is also the one place in the entire house that makes Brian's mother feel uncomfortable. Unfortunately, this is where they keep their freezer so she has to make regular trips to the basement, but she has never gotten used to the feeling in this area.

The video of this window is certainly a mystery, and I began to think of how many of the inexplicable sightings at the house actually involve windows. Solid figures and lights have only appeared to witnesses looking in or out of windows:

- When Larry was outside he saw the figure of a person standing inside by a window, as well as the winged animal in the basement.
- Brian's cousin was looking out through the attic window when she saw the crippled man going down the driveway.
- The video showed lights and eyes outside of the basement window.

What significance does this have, and why hasn't anything manifested to witnesses inside the house when they are inside, or out in yard when they are outside? The ghosts certainly haven't been shy about footsteps or shoving people and tugging on their legs, so why be so elusive with physical appearances? Unfortunately, it's another piece of the puzzle that will most likely remain unsolved, but it is certainly worth noting, and keeping in mind for any future encounters.

In the mean time, Brian, Larry and other family members will watch as stains, figures and lights appear and disappear, listen as things go bump in the night, and hope that there won't be any more violent physical attacks in this house that just might have windows that look into the other world...

Above- The photo I took in April of the stain as it appeared after Brian applied water. While it is clearly visible, it pales in comparison to the photo below, which Brian took in July when the stain appeared on its own, and disappeared after two days. Whatever triggers this darkening is stronger than mere water.

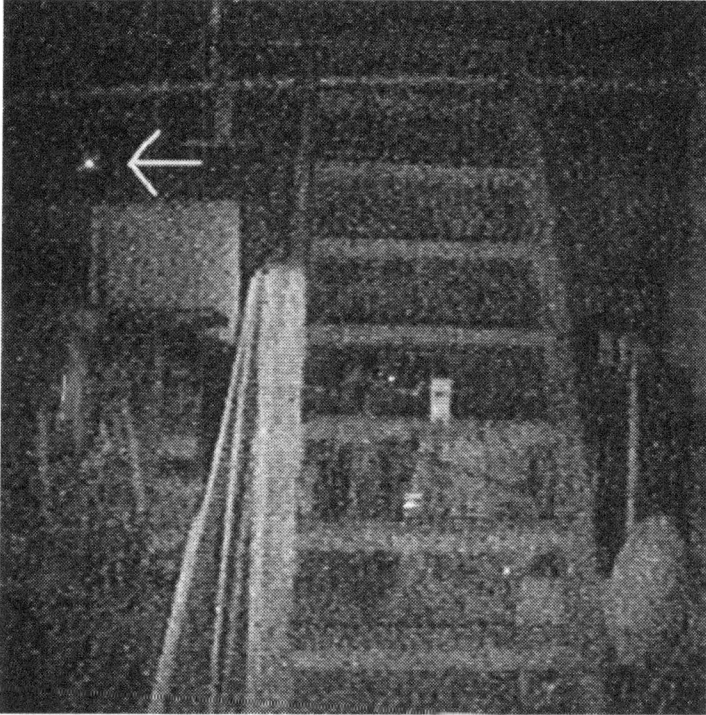

This infrared image shows one of the inexplicable lights (to the left of the arrow) that moved outside of the basement window. This was one of the single bright lights. The "eyes" were two less intense parallel lights that also moved along the outside of the window. None of the lights followed a straight path, they moved up and down and side to side at various heights and in different directions, and lasted for different lengths of time (none lasted more than several seconds.)

Home for Elderly Ladies Update

It has been four years since we first investigated the former "Home for Elderly Ladies" in Port Jervis (see *Ghost Investigator Volume II*). In that time the owner, Marie, has been hard at work completely renovating the place. In an effort worthy of a *This Old House* episode, the drab and decaying interior has undergone a remarkable transformation.

However, as the massive undertaking draws to an end and Marie's family prepares to move in, one vital question remains—has the house also undergone a paranormal transformation? As old walls came down and physical remnants of the past were removed, did the ghosts also leave the building?

One of the most common occurrences had been the sound of footsteps—a phenomenon for which I can personally vouch! During our first investigation, Bob, Mike and I were in the basement and clearly heard the footsteps of someone in hard-soled shoes walking on the floor above us. A plumber and his assistant had heard several people walking around when they were alone in the house. Marie often heard footsteps and odd sounds, as if the former inhabitants were curious about the new owner.

Would the curiosity of these phantom walkers continue during the renovations? Apparently they would…

While the vast majority of the work has been done by Marie's own skilled hands, she did hire two men to finish putting up some sheetrock on the first floor. As the men moved about on their stilts doing their work, they kept hearing what sounded like footsteps above them on the second floor. They were unaware of the ghostly reputation of the place, and knew they were supposed to be alone in the house, so the footsteps didn't make any sense. Could it be the sounds of their own movements echoing through the house? Finally, keeping very still, they realized that someone was definitely walking on the floor directly above them.

One of the workmen pulled off his stilts and ran out of the house in terror. Not knowing where Marie lived, he went across the street and asked a neighbor. The neighbor was able to give him Marie's address, where he promptly went to tell her that he quit because the house was haunted. Knowing what she did about the house, how could she argue with him!

The workman had one other thing to say—under no circumstances would he ever go back into that house, not even to get his tools. Sure enough, the man was good to his word and arranged a time to stop by and have Marie bring his tools out to him.

While this one incident stands out, Marie found that as work progressed, paranormal activity diminished. Perhaps the old ladies have accepted their new surroundings, or perhaps the physical changes in the structure have somehow broken the bond that tied them to the place. Or, possibly, they are simply saving their energy and waiting for the family to move in?

When we arrived one evening in March of 2005, we found that the exterior had also undergone quite a makeover. But no one had prepared me for what was inside. Had I been blindfolded and led into the house, I never would have recognized the place. Crumbling plaster walls, tiny rooms and years of grunge have been replaced with fresh paint and wallpaper, a more open floor plan, and something that makes this author's heart beat a little faster—theme rooms!

Maybe I've never really grown up, or maybe I'm not one to follow tradition, but having fun with themed decor just makes me feel like a little kid again. For example, I have to admit that in my home we turned a dining area into a retro diner—diner booth, jukebox, the whole nine yards. It's my favorite place in the house, and it's also the favorite spot of guests. So imagine my utter delight when I found that Marie had done something similar, only on a much larger scale!

Where once there were a couple of small bedrooms where little old ladies quietly spent their last days, there's now a large sports and game room replete with a picket fence along the wall to give the sense of being outdoors. There's the nautical bathroom, the Washington Redskins room (nice idea, but as a Giants fan I seriously question the choice of team!), and so on throughout several thousand square feet of new living space. The old creepy feelings that used to be in this section of the house are gone, as were any unusual EMF readings, sounds or images in photographs—at least during this latest investigation.

However, the basement hasn't changed much, either in appearance or feel. While we were down there, I heard a few banging and knocking sounds for which I was unable to determine a source. The strangest feelings were once again in that odd wooden-paneled room, which was part of the original structure built in the 1800s. (The addition was built in the early 20th century.)

An infrared image of Mike in the paneled room in the basement, where uncomfortable feelings are heightened by strange noises and unusual activity.

The instruments and cameras didn't pick up anything, but we were only down there for a few minutes. We hadn't planned another full investigation, thinking that there wasn't much remaining to investigate. I think we underestimated the place.

We went through the rest of the house, basement to attic, and the only room upstairs that seemed to have any paranormal activity that night was the bedroom where the mysterious voice had been recorded on our first investigation. Marie still refers to this place as the "creepy room," and it is here where children are drawn to the closet, happily closing themselves inside and laughing and talking for hours. (They have no such interest in any of the many other closets in the house.)

The voice I may have recorded there sounded like a female whispering, "There she is."

As we recalled that previous investigation, Mike joked that he would give me a dollar to stand in the closet with the door shut. As I obviously like a challenge, I went into the dark closet and closed the door. I had been laughing when I went in, but my mood changed very quickly. Almost immediately my skin started to crawl, and it really felt like someone was standing in there with me. I know this is not scientific evidence, but the presence was so intense and so distinct I could have sworn that someone was so close as to almost be up against my left side. I didn't ask Mike for that dollar, I was just happy to get out of there.

As this room is also part of the original 19th century structure, I started to consider the idea that even before the addition was built and a single elderly lady moved in, this place was haunted. Many locations I've investigated have layers of hauntings, and it seemed that even if the old ladies had left the newer section of the house, the original building may still have its ghostly occupants.

This story will no doubt continue, as the real test will come when the family moves in.

Body in the Basement?

When Karen first went to look at the small two-bedroom house for sale in Orange County, New York, she was delighted to find that it had a wonderful view of the lake that was just across the street. When she entered the former summer cottage, sunlight was streaming in through the windows, bathing the rooms in an inviting glow. Unfortunately, all that light was deceptive. There was a darkness in that house waiting to reveal itself...

At the closing, Karen's lawyer informed her that according to the law, the sale would be final—unless the place turned out to be haunted. She would have two weeks to make that determination, and if anything happened after that time it would be too late to do anything about it. In retrospect, it was a rather curious thing to say, but a closing is frightening enough, and Karen's mind was certainly not on ghosts as she signed the checks and contracts.

Moving day was at the end of April in 1998, and Karen and her teenage daughter, Jennifer, settled in—or at least they tried to. Just one week later, on May 5, their dogs started to act very strangely. They were scratching and sniffing at the door to the back bedroom, desperately trying to get in. The dogs were insistent, and acted as though someone, or *something*, was inside. Karen finally opened the door, and they darted into the room and ran back and forth, still sniffing the air and floor in their search for whatever it was they were looking for.

The dogs' behavior was so unusual, and so frantic, Karen thought that a squirrel must have gotten inside the house, or possibly in the walls. The home inspector she had hired prior to the closing had done a very thorough job, and had assured her that there weren't any mice or squirrels, but given the dogs' bizarre actions in this room, it seemed to be the only rational explanation.

It's too bad that it turned out that the term "rational" was not going to able to be applied too often in regards to what goes on in this house. It's also too bad that nothing else happened during those first two weeks, as the legal window of opportunity for getting out of the deal passed. Then it got *really* interesting.

Objects started falling. It began innocently enough with a loaf of bread coming off the kitchen counter. The first time something like that happens it seems odd, but it doesn't really register as anything paranormal. However, when other objects started falling off the shelves right in front of them, that was another story.

Another object that moved was a "love bead" that had been given to Jennifer by an ex-boyfriend. The iridescent piece of glass usually sat on a shelf, but after Karen made the beds in the morning, she would often find the bead conspicuously placed in the middle of Jennifer's bedspread. The shelf was not next to the bed, so even if the bead had somehow been knocked off the shelf, it would have ended up on the floor, not the bed. Neither Karen nor Jennifer ever saw the token of love being moved, but this was clearly another sign that something was trying to get their attention.

Then there was the musty, earthy odor. Although the house was built in the 1920s, it was structurally sound and there wasn't any mold or evidence of water damage. Yet, at times there would be a sudden and overpowering blast of stale air, reminiscent of strong smelling dirt—perhaps like the odor of something from a grave? This occurred several times throughout the house, most notably in the closet of the back bedroom, but the bad air would pass as suddenly as it came.

If there was a chronic mildew problem, the odor should be constant, not coming and going for brief moments, in different parts of the house. Still, the problem persisted. Years later after Karen remarried, her husband searched the attic above the closet and even removed part of the closet wall to look for signs of moisture. Everything was dry, and there were no odors inside the walls.

In addition to an earthy smell and objects moving, there was fire. Fortunately, it was controlled fire from the stove. Karen would often get up in the morning or come home from work and find one of the stove burners on. It was very frustrating and upsetting, and on one occasion she blamed her daughter for being irresponsible by not turning off the stove. Her daughter listened patiently to the accusation, then calmly replied that she hadn't even been in the kitchen that day. This went on for years, and finally Karen's husband, John, solved part of the mystery. However, in the process a deeper mystery was uncovered.

John was standing in front of the sink, which is adjacent to the stove. Right before his eyes, he saw the knob on the stove slowly *turn by itself*, and only stop when the gas was ignited and the flame appeared! If he had any doubts about the activity in the house, he began to become a believer that day.

In an attempt to finally end this dangerous paranormal prank, they removed the old stove and installed a new one. The knobs on this stove have to be pushed in and then turned, so a burner can't possibly ignite accidentally. Unfortunately, this activity is no accident, and the burners on the new stove still turn themselves on!

Then there is the high-pitched, ear-piercing sound that is so irritating it causes the family members to cover their ears. The sound is always accompanied by an unpleasant feeling, and it doesn't appear to have any logical source. One day the sound was coming from the stove, another day from a light fixture, and still another time from a stuffed toy. It comes, it annoys, it leaves, and nothing anyone does can stop it.

There are also colored lights, most notably orange, green and yellow. Sometimes they move out of the walls and cross the room. Sometimes they just appear and disappear in thin air.

While there were no explanations for any of these bizarre phenomena, it was obvious that the family was not alone in this house. Then one more addition to the household came along—a son, Justin, who very early on claimed to have some interesting "imaginary friends."

Young Justin told his mother that he played with "a boy in the dark" who came to see him. When she asked what it was like when he visited, her son hugged himself and shivered, and replied, "Cold, Mommy. It's very cold." In the past few years, Karen has seen a dark, shadowy figure, which she believes is the "boy in the dark" who speaks to her son.

Karen's first sighting was at night in a room that had a rack of stereo equipment with bright LED displays. The lamp in the room was not on, so the only light came from the stereo. As Karen entered, she realized that she could not see the light from most of the LED displays. Something was blocking the light, something tall, dark and very solid. In an instant it vanished, and the unobstructed stereo displays shone brightly again.

On another night, she walked into her son's room and saw the same tall, dark figure standing in front of the closet. She noticed more detail this time—the figure had broad shoulders, but was thin and angular. Karen compared the apparition with that of the classic image of Sherlock Holmes with his cloak across his shoulders.

Justin also has another playmate, a girl who just happens to be dead, but doesn't let that stop her from coming to visit Justin and the spirit of the boy. In a remarkable statement to his mother, Justin revealed that this girl "didn't die in the house," but that she had been killed by a truck when its brakes failed. Not exactly a toddler's typical imaginary friend!

Justin continued to make incredible statements like this, often concerning things that happened many years ago. He has displayed a familiarity with people and places that he should have no way of knowing about. He has given names and characteristics to the different colored lights. He has wondered out loud why the cartoon character Casper the Friendly Ghost is portrayed with such a large head, "because real ghosts don't look like that." Justin has also complained about the back yard—not because there wasn't a pool or a swing set— but because there weren't any grave markers!

Understandably, Karen was getting desperate at this point, and she consulted a priest hoping that he might perform a blessing in the house. He refused, and instead told them that they should simply ignore all the activity. That's easy to say when you don't have to live with objects moving, ear-piercing sounds, grave-like odors and your son's dead playmates!

She next consulted a psychic on the telephone, who suggested using holy water throughout the house. Placing the water in a spray bottle, she began distributing it in each room. Justin, who had been deeply absorbed in a television show, suddenly came running over to her in a state of extreme agitation, demanding to know what she was doing. Karen explained that she was just trying to get rid of cobwebs. The excuse did not appear to mollify the boy, as the next day he broke the spray bottle. He later accused her of being a "ghost killer."

It appeared to be time to have the psychic come to the house. His initial impression upon entering was that the place was like a spiritual "highway" of lost souls coming and going. He also felt that there were some souls there to stay—specifically a boy who had died on the property on May 5, 1912.

According to the psychic, the boy was playing with a gun and accidentally shot himself. His parents, who were strict Irish Catholics, found his body and called for their priest. The priest declared that it was not an accident, the boy had taken his own life, and therefore could not be given a proper burial in consecrated ground. The boy was buried on the property where he died, in an unmarked grave, and forgotten. The family also buried the terrible secret of the suspicious death, and never spoke about the boy again. Years later, the summer cottage was built over his grave, with the back bedroom being located directly above his remains beneath the dirt floor of the basement.

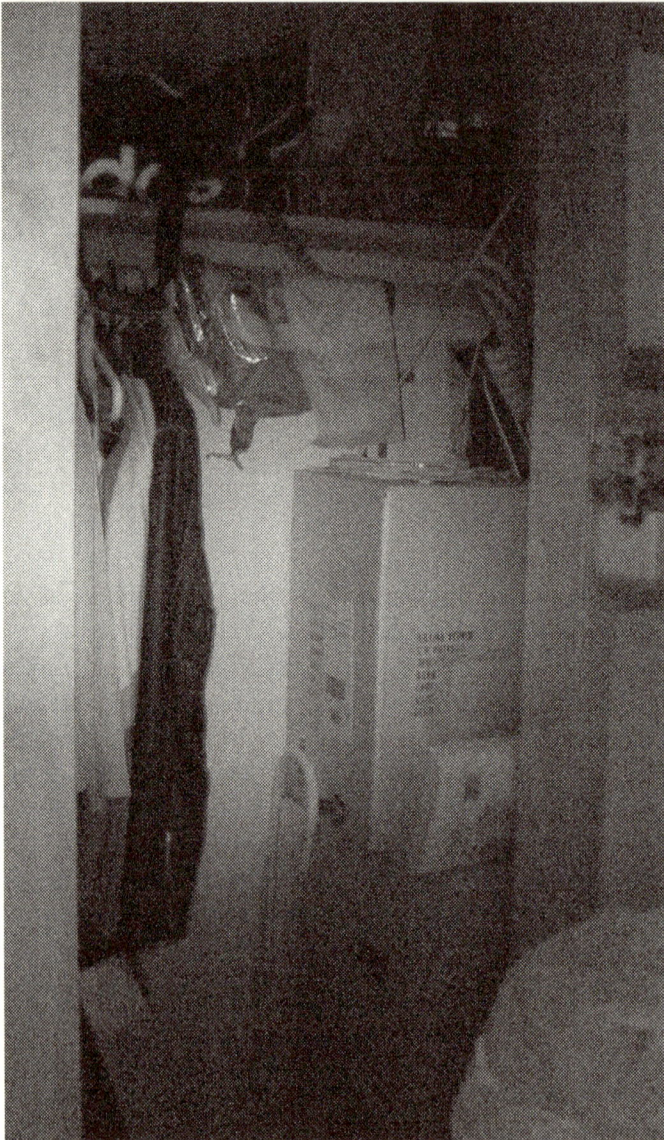

The closet of the back bedroom, which the psychic believes is directly over the site of the boy's remains in the basement.

Was this a fanciful tale compiled from pieces of information Karen had already given the psychic, or is it the painful truth of a young life tragically cut short, and an injustice that has remained a secret for 80 years?

The activity did begin on May 5, just one week after Karen moved in. There is evidence that the spirit of at least one boy is in the house. Much of the activity is centered in the back bedroom. Justin did complain that there weren't any grave markers in the yard. Compelling facts, but is there any documented proof that such a boy ever existed, and that he died on the property on that date?

As Karen began searching for answers at the local library, someone mentioned my name and said that I investigate cases such as this. She called me one Saturday in January of 2005 and told me some of her story. Obviously, I was fascinated, and arranged to visit the very next day, when her son would not be there.

The former summer cottage is currently undergoing a significant transformation—John has doubled the size of the ground floor with an addition to the back of the house, as well as a second story containing a large master bedroom with a balcony overlooking the lake. Such a bright and sunny place with a great view seems to be an unlikely location to be haunted, but if there's one thing I've learned over years of ghost hunting, it's that looks can be deceiving.

Entering through the new part of the house, I was enthusiastically greeted by the dogs. I felt perfectly at ease in this section. However, when I walked down the hall and entered the kitchen in the original part of the house there was a momentary twinge. Nothing too pronounced, but just enough to be noticeable—just enough of an odd feeling to suggest that *something* might be there.

I was there mainly to get an overview of the case in context with the house and property. However, I did get several high EMF readings that came and went, and could not be traced to any natural source. There was one other incident of particular note that occurred in the original basement.

When we first entered the basement, there didn't appear to be anything out of the ordinary. Several minutes later, we started to discuss the "boy in the dark" and a powerful musty odor hit us. It's important to note that the smell was *not* there when we first went in, and we were just standing in place, not moving anything or stirring up dirt, and the door was closed. Also, the unpleasant smell passed by us, moving from my left to right, and was gone in a few seconds. I spent some time afterward sniffing around the basement trying to find a source, but nothing down there smelled anything like that musty odor that was definitely a few paranormal steps beyond mere dirt.

Between what Karen had told me and my brief experiences with the house, I was almost certain that this was a genuine haunting, but admittedly I was not ready to accept the psychic's accounts and the stories of a little boy as the gospel truth. I would need a lot more evidence. I would need to see for myself what a psychic with no previous knowledge of the case would find.

Until another investigation could be arranged, Karen did some digging—of the document kind—at the local government records office. She was trying to ascertain whether any boys had been killed by a gunshot in the year 1912. Normally, you need a name to search death certificates, but obviously in this case the circumstances were rather unique, and no names were known. Instead, Karen had to look at each and every record to see the age and cause of death. It was very time consuming, and the year 1912 came up empty.

However, she did find something rather startling in 1905. It was not the right year according to the psychic, but it was certainly the right circumstance, and the matter of the burial was quite unusual. On all of the other records, the cause of death was explained and then the place of burial and the church or type of religious service was noted. In this one record involving the death of a 12-year-boy, it simply said that he died from a shotgun blast and was "buried in the hill." Unfortunately, it didn't say what hill, or whether or not the shotgun blast had been an accident, murder or suicide.

Karen's house is on a hill. The psychic did say the boy died of a gunshot. And both her son and the psychic did claim that this boy's spirit was upset that he was not given a proper burial with a service and a grave marker.

It's tempting to believe that this is documented evidence of a boy buried under the house, his angry spirit still seeking justice for over one hundred years. Unfortunately, temptation doesn't equal proof. It's a very large town and there is no indication on which of the many hills the boy was buried. Just because the circumstances of the death were not detailed, it doesn't mean that it was anything suspicious. Also, the psychic had been adamant about the fact that the boy's family was Irish Catholic, but this boy's name was German or eastern European.

It was all close, but no paranormal cigar—yet.

80

In February, Karen called to let me know that her son would be spending the weekend with her daughter, so we would have an entire night to conduct a full investigation. I made sure my husband, Bob, and fellow ghost investigator Mike Worden would be available, and then I contacted psychic Cyra Greene. We first witnessed Cyra's sensitive abilities at Mike's grandmother's house, and I felt both confident and comfortable about her being the right person with whom to work on this case.

I told Cyra nothing. I actually felt kind of bad just giving her an address and asking her to show up at a certain time, but I wanted her to enter this house with a completely clean slate. Only if she had absolutely no prior knowledge of this case could I attest to the credibility of her observations.

Bob, Mike and I arrived about 7pm. We set up various cameras and equipment in the house and in the basement. Nothing eventful occurred right away, although Mike did feel very uncomfortable as he walked into Justin's bedroom—as if there was a line across the room that he shouldn't cross.

I set an EMF meter in the closet in the back room of the old part of the house (located over the spot where the boy is supposedly buried), and set up an infrared camcorder facing the closet. I then left the room and closed the door so that the scene would be undisturbed. Later when I watched the tape, I found that there was one short burst of EMF that made the meter's needle move and caused the alarm to sound. There were also several banging sounds that seemed to be very close to the camera, but as we had gone upstairs at some point, I can't rule out that the sounds were possibly made by us walking on the floorboards above. (Although Karen later told me the new floorboards don't make any sounds at all.)

An hour went by very quickly and we all eagerly anticipated Cyra's arrival at 8pm. It was a bitterly cold and windy night, but Bob bravely volunteered to stand at the bottom of the driveway and wait for her, as it was easy to miss the place in the dark. As soon as Cyra entered the house, I turned on the tape recorder I was carrying, and Mike started capturing everything on video. We didn't want to miss anything.

After everyone was introduced, we got right down to business. Starting in the old part of the house, Cyra first went into the front room, then the back room that has the active closet (I had removed all the equipment, so it wouldn't appear to be a place of interest.) Her initial reaction in these two rooms was to experience a sense of fear, and she remarked how curious it was to so rapidly go from admiring the beauty of the house, to feeling that pervasive fear.

I found it particularly interesting when Cyra next began to enter Justin's room, but with no words or explanations, she turned around and left after taking just a couple of steps. The point at which she turned around was precisely the spot where Mike felt the "line" that shouldn't be crossed. Later, when I asked why she didn't go all the way into the room, she really didn't know, and hadn't consciously realized that she had stopped.

Next came the new master bedroom upstairs, which is truly a gem of both architecture and decoration. Once again, Cyra began by admiring the design of the place (and the big screen television, which we both agreed was perfect for football), but once again those warm feelings were suddenly overwhelmed by something dark and uncomfortable. The feelings almost brought her to the point of tears, and she said that there was a distinct presence that had just entered the room.

"Can you tell from what age group?" I asked. "Male or female?"

"Girl," Cyra immediately replied, then fell silent for a moment of contemplation before speaking again. "This is what I got at first. Tall, big girl, adolescent. At first it was comfortable in here, now it's not! Something strange. Very uncomfortable, almost sick in the stomach."

Cyra placed both hands over her stomach as if she was ill or in pain, and the discomfort was clearly visible in her features. She remarked again about the suddenness of the feelings, and was quite sure that this girl's spirit was not there when she first came into the house. Was this the same girl that Justin claimed had been killed by a truck and often came to visit?

Our next objective was the new section of basement, which was separate from the original basement. I was most curious about what Cyra might find in the two basements, but I have to admit I didn't know what to expect. Would she confirm what Justin and the other psychic had claimed, that somewhere beneath our feet lay the bones of a boy who died in an accident that was ruled a suicide? Or would she find nothing, or sense someone or something completely different? It was the ultimate test, a chance to validate a case unlike any other I had encountered before.

As we descended the stairs, I recalled earlier that I had said to Bob and Mike on the drive over, "I don't know what Cyra will find, but if she says there's a boy buried under the house I'll grab a shovel and start digging."

I guess I should have brought a shovel.

The new basement is neat and clean and not the least bit spooky—at least visually. To someone as sensitive as Cyra Greene, outward appearances have little to do with the energetic reality of a place. After just a few moments in the basement, Cyra began moving both hands back and forth over her heart, and spoke the following words:

"Heart. Palpitating. Oh my God, something happened here. Something *really* happened here. It's like a strong vibration."

Cyra walked to her right a few steps, but came right back to the spot where she felt the most intense energy. Then she spoke one of the most remarkable sentences I've heard in my entire ghost hunting career.

"I wonder if anyone is buried right here. *Right here.*"

So there it was. No prior knowledge, no lucky guess, no coincidence. Before my very eyes, this woman almost immediately felt the spirit from a body whose remains were beneath our feet. I glanced over to Mike and we needed no words to express our astonishment. But it got even better.

I kept my cool and calmly asked, "Do you have any sense of who, what, where?"

"Long and gangly," Cyra quickly replied, her hands moving up and down over her head, almost as if she was stretching or pulling dough. "Could be a boy. It's like an androgynous figure. It's very long, adolescent and tall and stretched and not very fleshed out."

There was another pause as Cyra continued to move her hands as if she was physically feeling the outline of the tall, thin figure. She became more certain that it was a boy, and then tried to compare his appearance to two other people, and then realized that both of these other people had died as a result of their own actions. This revelation seemed to startle her out of the somewhat trance-like state she had been in.

Opening her eyes and standing up straight, she announced, "Maybe it's a suicide!"

"Any sense of how he died?" I asked, still maintaining a curious, yet neutral countenance, which was becoming more difficult with each passing revelation.

"He...hurtled himself," Cyra said, her body making motions as though she was falling or being thrown. She also appeared puzzled and not completely clear as to what this initial impression actually meant. Then she suddenly raised a finger to her lips. "It was all hush, hush. It was a secret."

It was like frosting on the cake. Here were all the major elements of the story that had been brought to light by Justin and the first psychic. A boy dying under suspicious circumstances, his body being buried on the spot and his memory forgotten as the family kept it all "hush, hush." I had been waiting for seven years for a case like this, and here on that cold night in the basement of that house, I heard what amounted to as much of a confirmation as one is ever likely to hear in a ghost investigation.

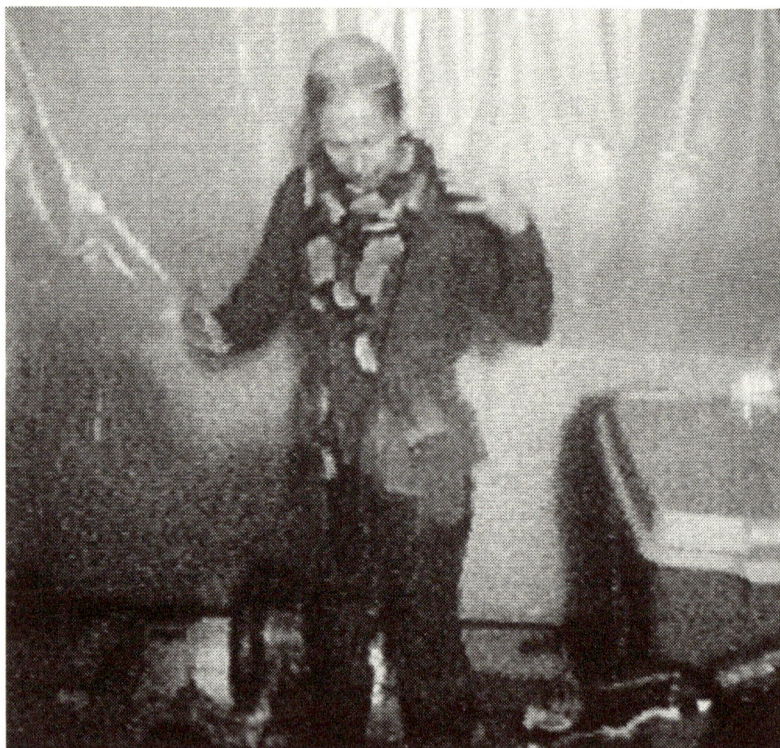

Cyra's attention is drawn to the floor as she describes the feeling that a body of a boy is buried beneath our feet. (Infrared image.)

I was very impressed. I was also practically busting at the seams to finally tell Cyra why I had asked her here.

"At this point," I began, "I think I can now tell you that the boy who lives in this house has been talking to the spirit of a boy whom he claims is buried under the house."

I also explained that both Justin and the first psychic had mentioned the accident/suicide scenario, the unmarked grave and the fact that everything was then kept secret.

Rather than patting herself on the back, Cyra's immediate reaction to this news was to be concerned for Justin.

"This could change the child's life—not knowing the difference in the divide between those who are alive and those who are not."

We discussed the implications of the situation, and we all agreed that this was not something to be ignored, as the priest had urged. But before we could plan any solutions, we needed more answers.

Cyra was drawn back to the spirit of the girl, and she reiterated that the girl was definitely *not* there initially, and that she "came to visit."

"This is a *site* haunt, rather than something haunting Karen and John," Cyra stated, emphasizing this crucial point. "This is clearly a site haunt."

This was important information for several reasons. For starters, it's always better to have a *place* haunted than a *person*. Obviously, no one wants a ghost to follow him wherever he goes. Also, in the case of a site haunting, you are investigating, and often subsequently trying to "treat," a localized area. Generally, these cases also involve a particular event or situation. Understanding this may not make a resolution any easier, but it's at least some comfort for the homeowners to know that if they leave, they will most likely leave their paranormal troubles behind. Unfortunately, that usually means the next unsuspecting owners inherit the ghosts.

"Any sense of how the girl passed?" I asked, hoping for more clarification to these muddy spiritual waters.

"It's connected," Cyra said without hesitation, referring to the idea that the girl and her death were somehow related to the boy and his passing. "It seems that this was really a hush, hush situation, and it's possible that they did the burial almost like being buried alive—'suffocated' kept coming to mind—but they kept him there."

Had the boy only been unconscious, perhaps in a coma, and mistaken for dead? If so, that would certainly not help a spirit to rest in peace.

"He was buried on this site?" I asked to reaffirm the assertion that this house was indeed built over a grave.

Cyra nodded her head in agreement, then said, "Very sad. Hush, hush going back generations ago. Very skinny frame, awkward. Long chest, seems longer than the legs. Eastern European. Polish? Slovakian? Bony face, skinny nose, prominent eyebrows."

As Cyra spoke her hands moved in front of her own features as if she was modeling a sculpture of the boy in clay. It was also interesting to note that she felt that the boy's family was from eastern Europe, not Ireland as the first psychic had felt. In 1905, the boy who had died of a shotgun blast had a Germanic name, but Cyra didn't know that.

In fact, as if to further put to rest the idea of him being Irish Catholic, she went on to specifically state, "*Not* Irish, Italian or Mediterranean. Ukraine? Two generations ago, about 100 years ago."

This would place the boy's death around 1905.

"Was it an accident?" Cyra asked, seemingly to no one visible. "He didn't die prepared. He wasn't ready.

Whatever it was, the girl thought she caused it and she always kept that a secret that she knew something. The girl was never the same after that. She kept a secret life, closed up. The secret was too big for her.

She hovered around his grave, so to speak. She was odd, considered a little bit of a mental case."

As fascinating as this information was about the dead, her insight as to the repercussions on the living were even more unnerving.

"I'll tell you that the child here [Justin] is getting very disturbed. He's becoming like this [like the dead boy and girl] and needs help.

Scary!

This child [Justin] likes the other world more. The spirits are very happy to have him. They love having him."

Again we paused for some discussion, and as anxious as Karen and John were to know what was happening, we decided to wait until Cyra was finished and then present all of the findings at once. Our next stop was the old basement.

Unlike the new basement, this area was cramped and dark, and still had much of its original dirt floor. Cyra was immediately drawn to the dirt area, but to physically be on top of that section she would have had to crawl. Fortunately, the feelings were strong enough where we stood that crawling wasn't necessary.

"Right here, just starting up, a heart feeling," Cyra began.

"An energy area, or a distinct individual?" I asked.

"Confusing…sexual," Cyra replied, struggling with a tangle of new thoughts and emotions. This was a provocative new concept—the possibility that these were not two innocent adolescent children. "I think I'm closer to the body, the original skeleton down here."

This agreed with the first psychic's belief that the boy's actual remains rested somewhere beneath that dirt.

"There's a connection with the girl, she's hovering around. The boy was blindsided. The look on his face! He was naked from the waist up like it was summer…something happened behind him…a rock hurled in jest?"

At this point I told her that the other psychic believed he was killed by a gunshot. She closed her eyes for a moment and then slowly shook her head "no."

"No gun. I don't see any gun. It was a natural object, something of the land. He fell. The girl was there. There were dry holes, like craters…earthy…dusty…rocky."

Karen had discovered a few weeks earlier that the land around her house had been subjected to heavy logging and mining, and almost all of the trees had been stripped from the landscape. It is likely that the landscape did appear cratered and dusty one hundred years earlier.

"It does seem accidental," Cyra continued as images and impressions streamed in. "There might have been horseplaying, and the girl was responsible. He could have provoked her to anger. His father was very strict, and nothing he did was right. He was very depressed. There may have been something sexual between the boy and the girl, something taboo. Was it his sister?"

There appeared to be no limit to the possible layers in this case, and I was beginning to think nothing would surprise me anymore. However, things were about to get very interesting—and personal.

Cyra moved away from the area near the dirt to between Mike and I near the door. She asked that the lights be turned out, as she wanted darkness and quiet to "look" more deeply, and make a stronger connection with the boy. While reviewing the videotape of this episode later, I thought that the eerie glow of Cyra's face in infrared and her remarkable words were startling. But believe me, the tape was nothing compared to actually standing in the darkness and listening to her give

87

voice to a spirit whose bones we may have been standing on at that moment.

"Ow!" Cyra said, cringing as though she had felt physical pain. "No, don't do that. Don't do that! Get outta here. Get outta here. Pick it up. Pick it up. Don't throw me. Don't throw me. Don't throw me."

By this point, I could sense a strong presence, and while it seemed as though Cyra might have been speaking words from an incident that occurred 100 years earlier, I also felt as though this entity was cognizant of the present. I started to consider directly focusing my thoughts toward communicating with him.

"What are you doing here?" Cyra demanded from her trancelike state, struggling to keep herself from shouting as the feelings of anger increased from the other side.

Was that comment directed at me? I felt my body tense at the possibility.

"Weasel, weasel, it's mine, it's mine," Cyra continued as if speaking from the past.

I relaxed, but only for a second.

"Where's my friend?" she again demanded, as I got the distinct impression that the spirit of the dead boy was not happy that we were there meddling in his affairs, and that his friend Justin was gone. "Who are you?"

This was getting personal. I could feel it.

"Get outta here! Get outta here!" Cyra said angrily, the line between the past and present blurring in the cold darkness.

However, unlike some entities who can be very intimidating and frightening, I didn't feel as if this boy had any power over me. I never experienced any of the fear and discomfort that Cyra and Mike had (not to mention Karen's family), and even as I stood in the old basement with cobwebs in my hair, with no lights, and listened to a hundred-year-old angry boy yelling at me, I felt nothing but a slight annoyance at this disobedient child.

Don't worry, it's okay, I thought to myself, trying to console the agitated spirit so that we might get more answers.

"*No, it's not okay!*" Cyra immediately blurted out within a second of my thought!

I think my eyes must have popped wide open in astonishment, and I was immediately convinced that the spirit of the boy could read my thoughts and was directly responding to me. Though surprised, I still felt no fear. Not that I am fearless—far from it!—but this spirit just did not affect me like he did others. Once in a while I get lucky.

I said nothing about what had just transpired, and just remained silent to see what else would unfold.

"You're just here to find something wrong!" Cyra continued, as the stress of the connection appeared to be taking its toll. It was doubtful that she could go on much longer. "Don't tell! Don't tell! Mean. Mean. Mean. Mean."

With that, Cyra took a deep breath and opened her eyes. The deep connection was broken—by her choice.

"I'm getting just an angry kid," she explained. "There's so much anger, and it's really hard because he's possessive and feels he can never do anything right. Mad all the time. Joyless.

Justin is getting all of this negativity, because these were angry people before they died, and he's getting assaulted with all of this anger. He's getting his role models from the dead."

The situation was even more serious than we first imagined.

Cyra, Mike and I went upstairs to look at some of Justin's drawings and attempts at writing. The first thing that struck us was how expressionless all of the faces were in every drawing. No smiles, not even any frowns—just straight lines for mouths. The figures he drew were also often accompanied by crosses. There were no scenes of happy children and flowers and sunshine like those that often line the walls of kindergartens and cover the fronts of refrigerators. These were somber, serious and disturbing.

As for the writing, Justin had repeatedly written down the same groups of letters, as if trying to spell something specific. One word looked like "Slovak" and others Cyra recognized as being sounds and syllables in Polish. The family is not from eastern Europe, and the child has not had any known exposure to the culture and languages of this region.

Finally, it was time to speak with Karen and John, who had understandably been waiting impatiently with Bob in the kitchen. It was interesting that when Cyra first arrived, she noticed an old metal colander hanging on the wall, and now used its image to help convey her meaning. She explained that Karen and her son, Justin, were open receptors, and had no filters to block anything from the other side. They needed spiritual colanders, something to block out the negative forces. Cyra had no doubt that there were at least the spirits of an angry boy and girl in this house, and that they were imposing their unhappy energies on the family.

We told them about everything Cyra had sensed, and when we got to the part about a boy being buried under the house, there was both a look of relief and alarm on Karen and John's faces. This was the confirmation they had been seeking, but as John had so aptly put it, "Great, so now what the heck do we do about it?"

Cyra spoke at length to John in private about his resistance and skepticism over the years. She felt that this only made the spirits more aggressive and determined to make their presence known, and it didn't help Justin in trying to deal with his difficult position of being caught between worlds. John agreed to try to be more open-minded, and not dismiss everything his son had been telling him.

Of course, this is all much easier said than done, and it works both ways for those who experience the paranormal, and those who do not. What is important in every case is to maintain a balance between keeping an open mind, and believing that *everything* is a sign of a ghost. The term "healthy skepticism" is often used to gently urge non-believers into judging the facts and not blindly discounting every shred of evidence. I would also urge "healthy reality checks" for those who are prone to letting their imaginations run wild.

In extreme cases such as this, where a particular spirit is so intrusive and may be negatively impacting the development of a child, it's even tougher to maintain a middle ground. The natural instinct is to protect your child, but when parents disagree as how to best accomplish that, there will be friction. I had great sympathy for Karen and John, and increasing irritation toward the angry spirits making their lives difficult. Life dishes out enough to us every day without having to deal with a few heaping servings of trouble from the dead.

While some spirits do need just a little help to move on, too many are angry and obstinate and won't budge, and don't care who they make miserable. I know I should always maintain a compassionate attitude toward lost souls, but damn it, why can't they deal with their own problems and leave innocent people alone?

(Okay, now that the Ghost Investigator has vented some of her frustration, I'll get on with the story.)

Cyra, Karen and John developed a plan of action. John would slowly begin speaking to Justin about his "friends." When he felt the time was right, he would then go into the old basement with his son and ask him to communicate with the spirit of the boy and find out what could be done to make him happy and have him move on to a better place. We would then return with Cyra and interview the boy and see what else we could find out. Ideally, this process could begin as soon as Justin came home on Sunday night.

Nice plan, but you know what they say about the best laid plans…

When Justin's sister brought him home the next day, he threw something of tantrum. He screamed and cried that he didn't want to live there anymore, and declared, "I hate America."

My reaction to hearing about this statement was identical to that of Karen and John—where did *that* come from? Were these the words of a 4-year-old boy who knows nothing of the world, or was this the angry statement of an immigrant child who had found no happiness in this country? Perhaps we had ruffled a few ghostly feathers during our investigation, and subsequent plans to try to remove the spirits from the premises.

The next day after things had calmed down, John causally asked his son, "You do know that your friend is dead?"

Justin was clearly pleased that his father was finally acknowledging his friend's existence, and happily answered, "Of course I know he's dead, Daddy, but you can't die twice, you know."

Another unusual statement from a 4-year-old, but what it meant remains a mystery.

Justin then became very sick and ran a high temperature for several days. Obviously, while he was in this feverish state it was not the time to question him, so the plan was delayed yet again. When he felt better, John went with him into the basement and asked some questions, but Justin was not forthcoming with any answers.

However, when I returned several weeks later, Justin had a stack of pictures he had drawn of all his spirit friends—four of whom had their bodies buried on or near the property—and immediately launched into vivid and detailed descriptions of each of them.

First, there is the boy who fell, rolled down the hill and hit his head. He died on the spot and is buried somewhere under the house. Justin repeatedly referred to this boy as his friend, and drew him with one arm shorter than the other. I didn't really notice—as you don't expect anatomically accurate limb dimensions in a little boy's scribbled drawing—but Justin specifically pointed out the arm and declared that it was shorter because of disease.

"Now his ghost lives here and I first met him when I was three," Justin stated as if this was all perfectly normal.

Actually, he had been communicating with someone before he was three, but only learned his invisible friend's name at that point.

He then showed me pictures of this boy's parents, his girlfriend and her family. He continued to be very specific about the particular characteristics of each person—for example the girlfriend's unusually prominent cheekbones and dark circles under her eyes. At one point, I mistakenly started labeling a copy of one of his drawings with the wrong information, and he became very agitated that I had mixed up these people. It was clear he had a very deep and personal connection with them, and wanted to make sure I got the story right.

Then there was the Indian who had been killed by several men near a tree in the front of the property. The first psychic had identified that spot as a location where a death might have occurred and a spirit was lingering.

There's also a bad guy with a gun. Again, Justin was very specific that it wasn't a small gun you hold in your hand. It was a longer gun that you needed two hands to hold.

I asked where his friend was buried, and without hesitation Justin replied that the boy was under the old basement. Karen and I went into the basement with him, and he pointed to the exact spot—which just happened to be right where Cyra had also indicated she thought the boy had been buried.

I asked Justin if his friend would talk to me, and he said it wasn't possible because I didn't have the "special powers" to hear him, even though I "knew a lot about ghosts." He further explained that he doesn't speak out loud with his friend, they communicate in his mind because his friend's voice box broke when he died.

At this point, there was one thing of which I could be certain—I had never had a conversation like this before, let alone with a preschooler!

Was his friend happy, I wondered?

"No, he's unhappy because he doesn't have a bed to sleep in. He sleeps on hard rock," Justin replied, as I thought about John's description of the layer of bedrock that lay several feet beneath the dirt.

Didn't he want to move on to heaven?

"He can't go because he died here and stayed forever."

Was there something I could do to help him move on?

Justin paused and closed his eyes for a moment, as if having a silent conversation.

"He said yes."

What could I do for him?

"Well…If you want to do something, you have to dig a hole down there, and if you find his skeleton you have to bring him up and bring him to a doctor to see if he could do something. Then we could bring him back from the bone doctor and he would be all fixed up, because you have to build him because his bones are messed up."

"He wants his bones back the way they were?" I asked, imagining what a terrible fall would have done to a young boy's body. "That will make him happy and he'll move on?"

"Yeah, his spirit is all right, just his bones are broken."

"So, then he wants us to dig up his bones?"

Justin paused a moment, and his expression suddenly changed.

"No, he won't like it…He likes to be alone…He doesn't want you to mess up his home."

Apparently, the prospect of finally revealing this boy's remains—and therefore possibly causing him to move on—was something he didn't want to have happen after all.

I had hoped we might get some kind of sound recorded on tape, so I suggested we all be quiet and concentrate for a minute and see if his friend could get the energy to say something we could hear. There were several seconds of quiet, then two short tapping or clicking sounds that I didn't hear at the time, but were recorded on the tape. Immediately after those strange sounds, Justin declared, "He just said something."

The timing was certainly right, but was there anything to the sounds? Later I amplified and examined them on the computer, but could detect nothing intelligible.

As a final question, I asked if there were any messages for me, if any of the spirits wanted to tell me something.

Justin quickly said that there was one message from his friend.

"He wants you to know that he had a busted life, and when I was born he was in the basement buried forever until I grew up then his spirit came up."

I took a moment to think about this, then I commented that I hoped that after all this his friend would decide to go up to heaven. As remarkable as all of his other statements had been, I was not prepared for what Justin was about to say.

"If my friend doesn't go up to heaven, when I die and get my spirit and he doesn't go to heaven by the time I die, I'm staying here with him!"

93

If I was alarmed by this, I can only imagine how Karen felt when she heard her son declare his intentions. Immediately, we both told him that he should not stay. Tears welled up in his eyes and he insisted that he would never leave his friend. We decided we needed to quickly change this dangerous subject. We talked about ordinary things for a while and the tense moment passed.

Where does this case stand as of this writing, in August 2005? Still waiting for the opportunity to start digging.

There are several things to consider before this can happen. First, there's the mess and disruption of having one's basement dug up. Then it needs to be done while Justin is not there, as it will likely stir up a paranormal hornets nest which could greatly upset him.

Last, but certainly not least, we must consider what to do if a human skeleton is unearthed! By law there has to be an official investigation—police, medical examiner, perhaps more digging—with further disruptions for the family.

I know it's easy for me to say (especially since this isn't my house!), but I am firmly convinced that there is sufficient evidence to warrant a search. I'll even go one step further and say that we are morally obligated to dig for human remains at this site. If there's even a slight chance that the eternal fate of at least one lost soul hangs in the balance, then I am ready, willing and able to roll up my sleeves and dig for the truth.

Are the broken bones of a boy who died on this spot a hundred years ago somewhere beneath the dirt in this basement? (Infrared image.)

**To contact Cyra Greene
please send email to:**

cyraseer@hotmail.com

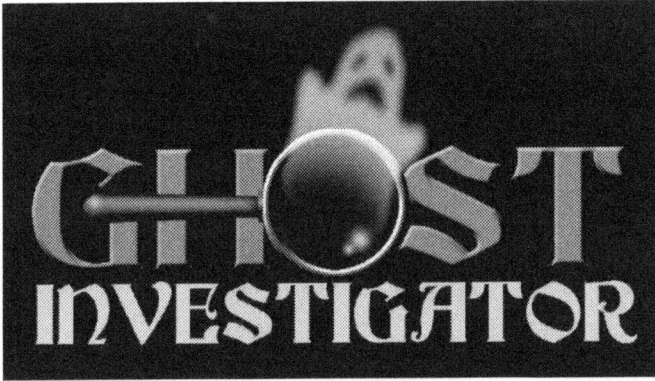

To order books, get info, and share your haunting,
contact the Ghost Investigator through:

www.ghostinvestigator.com

Or write to:

Linda Zimmermann
P.O. Box 192
Blooming Grove, NY 10914

Or send email to:

lindazim@frontiernet.net

Copy this page to use for your own ghost hunt. If you know of a haunted site you think should be considered for an upcoming book, please contact me at:
P.O. Box 192, Blooming Grove, NY, 10914
www.ghostinvestigator.com

Field Report

Date: Location:

Time In: Weather:

Names of People Interviewed:

Equipment: Camera   ☐ Video   ☐ Tape Recorder
                    ☐ Thermometer   Other:

Experiences: Sounds ☐   Odors ☐   Cold Spots ☐

      Visuals ☐ Touch/Sensations ☐ Movement ☐

Details (Attach extra sheet if necessary):

Time Out: Total Time on Site:

Conclusions:

Prepared and Signed by:

Witness(es):

Other books by Linda Zimmermann

Ghost Hunter Novel

Dead Center

When one of the country's largest shopping centers is built in Virginia, rumors abound that the place is haunted by ghosts of Civil War soldiers. Ghost hunter Sarah Brooks must uncover the truth, and come face to face with the restless spirits that walk through the *Dead Center* :

Okay, Sarah Brooks. This is what you do, she said to herself. *This is who you are.*

Closing her eyes, Sarah spun around and counted to three. When she opened her eyes, she had to clamp her hand over her mouth to stifle a scream. There was a pale, misty shape of a man drawing closer. It was like an image being projected into a fog, and it rippled, wavered, then slowly began to take on a more defined shape. The wounded man behind her screamed as if Death himself was coming to take him…

Science Fiction Novels

Mind Over Matter

Ten wealthy, powerful members of the Upper Circle rule the Union with an iron fist, and a small chip implanted in every citizen. Born to the privileged class, Walter Danan is now a wanted man. He has discovered extraordinary powers with which he hopes to break the council's grip and set mankind on a higher path of *Mind Over Matter*.

"Classic space opera!" Ernest Lilley, Editor, *SFRevu*

Home Run

On the fast track to becoming a baseball superstar, Rick Stella's injury leads him to join the Pioneer program for a year-long mission. Pioneers are sent into the farthest depths of space to start colonies, and are often never heard from again.

When Rick becomes marooned with his android crew, he must decide whether he is willing to sacrifice his dreams, or risk everything trying to make it home.

"Linda Zimmermann shows why she's an All-star in combining a story about baseball & SF to remind us how to overcome obstacles to emerge a winner!" Tony Tellado, *Sci-Fi Talk*

History

Civil War Memories "An exciting compilation of vignettes which bring Civil War history alive." Alan Aimone, USMA West Point

Forging a Nation "Linda Zimmermann blends the history of a single family with the history of our nation in its formative years. This is a story of patriotism, privilege and tragedy which touches the heart, and gives the reader a fascinating and very personal window into the past."
William E. Simon, former U.S. Secretary of the Treasury

"A worthy book." Arthur Schlesinger, Pulitzer Prize winning author/historian

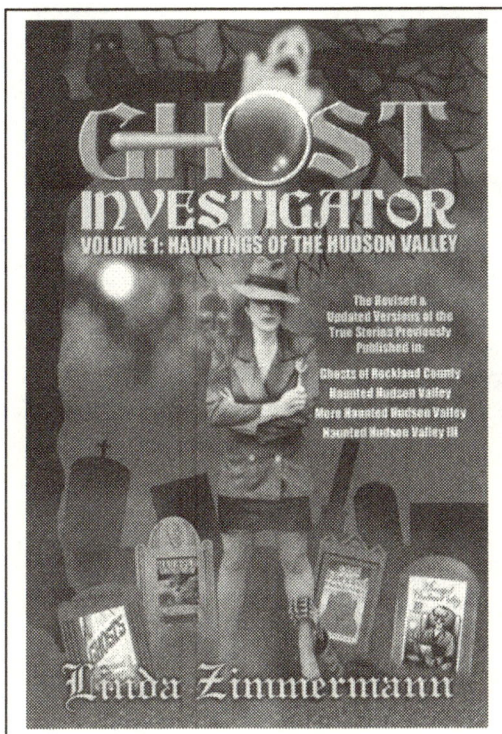

Ghost Investigator
Volume I
Hauntings of the Hudson Valley

Revised and updated true stories previously published in:

Ghosts of Rockland County
Haunted Hudson Valley
Haunted Hudson Valley II
Haunted Hudson Valley III

Readers' reviews from Amazon.com :

"If you live in the Hudson Valley area and you like true ghost stories, these books are a must have!"

"I had goosebumps the whole time and I was scared to go to sleep."

Ghost Investigator Volume 2
From Gettysburg, Pa to Lizzie Borden, AX

Ghost Investigator Volume 3

Ghost Investigator Volume 4
Ghosts of New York and New Jersey

Go to
www.ghostinvestigator.com
for photos, excerpts and to order these books.

"If you really want to get the feeling of what it's like to actually go 'ghost hunting' in cemeteries, cellars and abandoned buildings, you will love this book."

"Linda Zimmermann's books are among the most frightening I've read."

www.ingramcontent.com/pod-product-compliance
Lightning Source LLC
Chambersburg PA
CBHW031324040426
42443CB00005B/207